THE
RENEWAL
OF
THE
MIND

THE
RENEWAL
OF
THE
MIND

By John L. Sandford and R. Loren Sandford

Victory House Publishers
Tulsa, Oklahoma

Scripture quotations employed in the text are from the following versions: King James, Revised Standard Version, New American Standard and New International Version. All are used with permission.

Cover Design by Sandra Dalrymple

DEDICATION

To our friends of more than twenty-five years,
Ken and Donna Campbell

Ken is the manager and president of Elijah House. He establishes our schedule, runs the business of Elijah House, conducts the meetings, and wrestles through the days and in the long nights to dream up and think through the countless details and plans so needed to keep Elijah House moving forward to accomplish the purposes for which our Lord has called us into being.

Donna is the secretary who answers the phone and discerns what applicants for counseling ought to see which counselors, answers the mountains of correspondence, copies our teaching videos for VCR's, and counsels and prays for people over the phone when they interrupt her work.

Together they run Elijah House so well that Paula and I never have to give the home front a second thought while we travel and teach around the world; our minds and hearts are free to minister because they are in charge.

In gratitude and love, I dedicate this book to them.

Table of Contents

Acknowledgments   9
Foreword by Tom Stipe   11
Introduction   17

Section 1: Dethroning the Carnal Mind   23
  Chapter 1: Keeping the Beast Dead   25
  Chapter 2: Comprehending the Way
    the Lord Heals   43
  Chapter 3: Developing Mental Disciplines
    and Habits of Constant Prayer   53
  Chapter 4: Prayer Groups and Service   67

Section 2: The Depths of the Problem   75
  Chapter 5: Deep Ruts   77
  Chapter 6: Inherited Roots and
    Consequent Ruts From Adam and Eve's
    Sins in the Garden of Eden   89
  Chapter 7: Roots and Ruts Devolved
    From Adam and Eve's Sinful Replies
    to God in the Garden of Eden   119
  Chapter 8: Restoring the Functions of
    Mind and Heart, by R. Loren Sandford 145
  Chapter 9: Right Thinking About the
    Church and Authority,
    by R. Loren Sandford   161

Section 3: The Solution   195
  Chapter 10: According to Thy Word   197
  Chapter 11: Letting God Love Us   213

Acknowledgments

Our oldest son, Loren, contributed far more than chapters eight and nine of this book. His insights and sermons expanded our awareness time and again during the writing of these pages. In the latter half of 1989, while the book was gestating into its final form, Loren found new depths of pressing into Jesus, and his subsequent sermons breathed new life into our own devotions and worship and all our thinking.

Our son-in-law, Tony Lincoln, spent diligent hours trying to pare down my rambling wordiness into readable material.

Countless brothers and sisters in Christ have given us timely gentle and not-so-gentle reproofs over the years, and for the discipline that forced us into, I am most grateful. "Iron sharpens iron, so one man sharpens another" (Prov. 27:17). Without the corrections of my brothers and sisters, I would still be fumbling about in the darknesses of my carnal mind far more than I yet am. Much of the contents of this book owe their origin to the lessons learned in sharing with the Body of Christ, and returning to revamp my mind and heart into alignment with our Lord's ways, according to what encounters with others revealed.

Paula was at work writing *Healing Women's Emotions* as I composed this book, but she took

valuable time to read and edit and suggest, refining
my work within her unique kind of wisdom.

Finally, hundreds of loving Christians
responded to our pleas, in our Elijah House
Newsletters and appeal letters, donating their hard-
earned cash so that we could have more time to
write. I feel deeply the blessing of their choosing
to give so that this work might continue, and want
to thank all for their generous support.

No acknowledgment and thanksgiving could
be considered complete, however, so long as praise
and thanks have not been rendered to our
wonderful, gracious Lord and Friend, Jesus Christ,
the Son of God and our Brother. This last six
months have been the best of our Christian walk,
as He has wooed us daily more and more to love
Him first, last and always. What a joy and blessing
it is to know Him, and to realize that He has saved
the best wine for the last — both here in this life
and in the ages of blessing to come in heaven.

John L. Sandford

Foreword

Some months ago, John and Loren Sandford called and said they had a lengthy layover here in Denver, at Stapleton International Airport, and asked if I would like to use the time for some fellowship and conversation. Recognizing it as an opportunity to get better acquainted with new friends, I arrived in time to meet their incoming flight.

After finding a comfortable spot to settle down and talk for a while, we shared stories and discussed recent observations of the work of the Holy Spirit in the Church today. While comparing notes between John's inner healing ministry and my experience in Vineyard conferencing activity, as well as the day-to-day experience of church life, we observed a possible trend — Christian people having powerful encounters with the Holy Spirit, touching the innermost parts of their hearts and souls in our church services, conferences, counseling offices and other settings.

We had observed, with some consistency, people being overcome by honest emotion, grief, sorrow, remorse and, on some occasions, a seemingly uncontrollable wailing connected to some awful root of pain. Any pastor, counselor or ministry-team member worth his salt would immediately conclude that some kind of healing was taking place deep in the inner man, and would immediately, with compassion, begin praying for God's love, power, and mercy to comfort and bring wholeness to the individual in need. In light of the fact that this dialogue was taking place with a major spokesman and practitioner in the area of inner healing, the discussion got lively as we began to delve deeper into the subjects at hand.

During the personal interview process that often follows an individual's profound spiritual experience, I have found that messages, ministry times, worship in a public meeting or in the privacy of a biblical counseling session provide opportunities for the individual to get in touch with or be touched by the unresolved memory of sin committed against them, or sin committed against others. In many cases it seems that the Holy Spirit initiates the grieving process that so often represents the beginning of emotional healing.

These apparently sovereign moments bring for the minister and the recipient the hope for immediate, long-lasting change and on some occasions these individuals who experienced such "power encounters" were known to walk in new freedom and strength in their relationships with Christ. On many other occasions, however, these episodes brought no instant relief at all; rather they represented the beginning of a serious contest and lengthy battle with the results of sin and its residue.

In my meeting with John and Loren, a question came up that guarantees to make any

three-and-a-half hour layover at Stapleton pass
quickly: How do the frequent miracles of emotional
healing fit in with the sometimes fearful process
and discipline of confession and forgiveness? The
book you are about to read deals squarely with
those seasons, when the Holy Spirit sovereignly
and sometimes gradually reveals the effect of sin
in our lives and lays it on the altar of confession.
"If we confess our sins, he [God] is faithful and just
to forgive us our sins" (1 John 1:9). Though this
passage is commonly applied to the new convert,
it is quite probable that the way into the kingdom
is also the way to keep on progressing in the
kingdom. Getting in touch with one's sin is the
beginning point of God's faithfulness, as further
illustrated in the first chapter of First John. Feeling
the effects of sin done against you is the starting
point of God's justice. Most counselors and
ministers know that true grieving is the beginning
of healing and not necessarily an end in itself. But
a lack of understanding of the nature of confession
and forgiveness has led to more than one victim
of chronic emotional problems in the Body of
Christ.

John and Loren's book — *The Renewal of the
Mind* — is a closer look at renewal of the mind from
the miracles of immediate deliverance to the labors
of repeatedly ridding ourselves of the sin that so
easily besets us. "This is the message we have
heard from him and declare to you; God is light;
in him there is no darkness at all. If we claim to
have fellowship with him yet walk in the darkness,
we lie and do not live by the truth. But if we walk
in the light, as he is the light, we have fellowship

with one another, and the blood of Jesus, his Son, purifies us from all sin. If we claim to be without sin, we deceive ourselves and the truth is not in us. If we confess our sins, he is faithful and just and will forgive us our sins and purify us from all unrighteousness. If we claim we have not sinned, we make him out to be a liar and his word has no place in our lives" (1 John 1:5-9, NIV). For John the Beloved to sum up his entire life message in one metaphorical phrase, certainly draws my attention to its meaning. If God is light and we are privileged to walk next to Him in daily fellowship, certainly exposure of sin will be a natural, if not daily part of that experience.

There is another way to look at First John 1:7, "But if we walk in the light, with Him behaving as light behaves, we embrace the awesome prospect of being loved by a Father who will carefully and consistently shine His light into the deepest recesses of our being!"

Paul's prayer for us in Ephesians 3:16 is, "that out of His glorious riches he may strengthen you with power through his Spirit in your inner being, so that Christ may dwell in your hearts through faith." He further prays in Ephesians 3:18 that, "[We] may have power, together with all saints."

It is quite possible that in order to know the height and depth and length and breadth of the love of Christ that we will be known by Him at the deepest levels of our being. To know and be known at this level of godly relationship that surpasses knowledge means fully embracing the mystery and the majesty of a relationship with God that cleanses the heart and renews the mind.

By the time we had finished our lengthy airport discussion, I realized that John and Loren had already been giving the material presented in this book serious prayer and consideration. Hearing it conversationally was an inspiring preface to that which was to come. I encourage you to receive with great blessing, encouragement and exhortation the thoughts contained within these pages.

During the 80's Christian bookshelves declared the benefits of self-discovery and determining "who we are in Christ." My hope is that in this decade we will discover the reality of "who He is in us."

— Tom Stipe
Senior Pastor
Vineyard Christian Fellowship
Denver, Colorado

Introduction

I urge you therefore, brethren, by the mercies of God, to present your bodies a living and holy sacrifice, acceptable to God, which is your spiritual service of worship. And do not be conformed to this world, but be transformed by the renewing of your mind, that you may prove what the will of God is, that which is good and acceptable and perfect. (Rom. 12:1,2)

Our minds are like computers. Once the mind has ingrained a way of thinking, it maintains a kind of inertia, an habitual track it never leaves, unless jolted or forced off track.

Years ago, as a young pastor, I served a congregation which included many elderly shut-ins. It was a delight to listen to their stories as I made the rounds serving communion. One little old lady told me an identical set of stories at least forty times a year! It never ceased to amaze me, as she told and retold the stories of her years as a foreman in a silk factory, that she never seemed to realize she had repeated those same accounts hundreds of times before! Forty times a year I heard how she outwitted her biased, stupid boss! Each time the routine was identical, as though a needle had been dropped onto the groove of a phonograph record! — I heard the same inflections, pauses, intakes of breath, nods and giggles, and hands to the mouth in mock surprise.

Those pastoral visits began to disturb my liberal (at that time) bandwagon, which had trumpeted the realities and virtues of freedom of thought. Like many liberals, I had believed that I was the master of my own thoughts, that I could freely study a matter and objectively arrive at conclusions and consequent actions. The supposed freedom of the rational mind to cogitate, decide and philosophize had been eulogized and trained into us from earliest Sunday schools to the previous Sunday's sermon. I might have been able to rationalize that stages of senility had locked some of my elderly parishioners onto their tracks, had I not been shaken often in dealing with committees of alert, intelligent, healthy people in their prime. It had stunned me to watch educated, well-mannered "Christian" people give their services to the Lord, unaware that their ideas, methods and motivations were often saturated in and circumscribed almost totally by secular humanistic modes of thought! That realization was part of what caused me to become a most conservative evangelical!

Since then, in thirty years of counseling, Paula and I have seen that it is habitual tracks of the mind which defeat the fruits of counseling more than anything else. We discovered the hard way that it is not enough to wash long forgotten sins in the blood, nor enough to apply the cross to habitual patterns of *behavior.* The *mind* must learn to *think* in new ways. Habitual tracks of thought must be overcome before the new way of Christ can be built.

"Where the Spirit of the Lord is, *there* is liberty" (2 Cor. 3:17b, italics mine). Inversely, where His Spirit is *not*, there is *no* freedom.

Paula and I finally came to see that the carnal mind is not capable of true objectivity. Our minds are informed either by the Spirit or from the cesspools of the flesh!

> For those who are according to the flesh set their minds on the things of the flesh, but those who are according to the Spirit, the things of the Spirit. For the mind set on the flesh is death, but the mind set on the Spirit is life and peace, because the mind set on the flesh is hostile toward God; for it does not subject itself to the law of God, for it is not even able *to do so*; and those who are in the flesh cannot please God. (Rom. 8:5-8, italics mine)

Every Christian must deal with a two-fold problem in his mind. First, he must root out and destroy the practiced tracks of thinking he may never have realized are bondages. Without help he cannot do this. Secondly, he must seek new rootage in the Spirit, in the mind of Christ.

St. Paul said, ". . . we have the mind of Christ" (1 Cor. 2:16b). What a blessed truth. A fact! His mind *is in us!* But the carnal mind does not surrender its rule easily.

The mind of Christ in us is a fountain of eternal wisdom and freedom of thought. But *we must let go the old tracks of thought and learn to sink our roots into Jesus and build ways of letting His mind fill all the channels of our thinking processes.* It is the "how to" of that learning which is the subject matter of this book.

It is no easy task to transform all our thinking according to the Word of God. It involves both exterior and interior warfare. Our carnal mind is a Herod which would kill the Christ-child being formed in us if it could only discern where and how.

Early in life we assigned to our minds the task of guarding and keeping all our ways. Now that we are born anew and have invited the Holy Spirit to rule us, our carnal mind does not willingly relinquish its rule. Rather, the servant becomes the master, and like the man of lawlessness, our carnal mind "...takes his seat in the temple of God, proclaiming himself to be God" — "we," being the temple of God (2 Thess. 2:4, RSV).

Psychologically, the first task of our minds is not to think or to plan or regulate. It is to block out. In the present moment countless stimuli bombard us — from our seats, the lighting, sounds in the house, worries nagging at the back of our consciousness, heat and cold, hungers, thirsts, aches and pains, etc. If our mind did not block out most stimuli and decide which to heed and act upon, we would be in intolerable chaos — trying to respond to hundreds of stimuli all at once! *Our death on the cross at conversion poses utter threat to that ruling carnal center of decision-making within us.*

The real issue of the baptism of the Holy Spirit is not the gifts we receive nor even initially what fruits we can produce. The important thing is *who is in control.* The struggle is for headship. It is for this reason that the most brilliant are often the last to receive the baptism of the Holy Spirit. Their minds employ more arsenals of cleverness to avoid loss of control to the rule of the Holy Spirit! The primary purpose of the Holy Spirit is to install Jesus as Lord in every area of our lives. The baptism of the Holy Spirit does not therefore end the mental war — it begins it! (See Romans 7:22-25.)

For the reader, each chapter in this book may be far more than an intellectual exercise. It will likely be a game of "upset the fruit basket," in which the carnal mind must learn *not* to find a chair to be comfortable in, but to be aced out again and again, until it loses the game entirely, and has no place from which to sit and rule. It may be an invitation to conflict — and death.

Our carnal mind is often the last enemy to die within us. Jesus came to deliver all those who "Through fear of death were subject to lifelong bondage" (Heb. 2:15, RSV). It is not physical death we fear. That for Christians would be release and reward. *The death we fear is death of self.* It is not so much the death of bad practices we have come to see as destructive to our witness that we fear either. We long for that death too, even though fear twinges the process. It is the threat of death to our supposed self-control, our carnal mind's predominance over all that we think and do, fear of what awful things we suspect we might do if we let go — that is what chains us to the lifelong bondage of our fleshly ways of thinking! It is significant that Jesus was crucified upon Golgotha, "the skull," the residence of the mind, the first and last residence of sin in mankind.

The process of dying to our carnal mind's rule of us is like being asked to jump off a cliff with seemingly no guarantee of hands to catch us and hold onto us. We want to cry out, "Is there anyone else up there we can talk to, Lord?" But the paradox is that whoever hangs onto his life at this point loses it (Matt. 16:25), for when we maintain carnal, mental self-control, we reinstall self upon the throne and succumb to Satan's first temptation all over again!

Whoever lets go finds true freedom. Even the least intellectually gifted finds true brilliance and wisdom, for the mind set on the Spirit truly is attuned to "the things of the Spirit."

Section 1
Dethroning the Carnal Mind

1

Keeping the Beast Dead

This I say therefore, and affirm together with the Lord, that you walk no longer just as the Gentiles also walk, *in the futility of their mind,* being *darkened in their understanding,* excluded from the life of God, *because of the ignorance that is in them,* because of the hardness of their heart; and they, having become callous, have given themselves over to sensuality, for the practice of every kind of impurity with greediness. But you did not learn Christ in this way, if indeed you have heard Him and have been taught in Him, just as the truth is in Jesus, that, in reference to your former manner of life, you lay aside the old self, *which is being corrupted in accordance with the lusts of deceit,* and that *you be renewed in the spirit of your mind.* (Eph. 4:17-23, italics mine)

"And the axe is already laid at the root of the trees; every tree therefore which does not bear good fruit is cut down and thrown into the fire" (Matt. 3:10). Roots lie beneath the surface. In *The Transformation of the Inner Man* and in *Healing the Wounded Spirit,* we taught how to lay the axe to the roots of our sin nature. Others have taught well about the same things. Many have been set free. But too many have returned to their sins. When we cried out "Why?" the Lord answered that many have never fully understood the way of His healing nor grasped the necessity to wage warfare to overcome continuing habits of thoughts and feelings, nor the need to build new ways of thinking and feeling.

The Depths of the Battle

Few have yet comprehended the depths of the battle to renew the conscious mind. It is not merely a matter of *deciding* to change the way we think. Our mind owns deep ruts — long-practiced ways of thinking which are not overcome that easily. What so often has happened has been that when our counselees have begun to talk in new ways, we have celebrated, "Aha! They've got it!," but many times it was not so. Their conscious minds had begun to find new tracks, but the old ruts had never been fully dislodged. Much akin to a newly overhauled engine, the new rings of thought had not yet had time to seat themselves, so in the pressures of life, the motor blew the new and returned to the familiar tracks of the old. *Behind that was the carnal mind, seeking to regain control.*

Fred came because he could not cease being insanely jealous of his wife. True enough, she was an exceptionally beautiful woman and men were quick to notice her. Though she protested she was not doing anything to provoke their interest and couldn't help what they were doing, he would fly into accusatory rages: "You're flirting, making men pay attention to you!" "You want to go to bed with these guys — they're picking that up from you and coming on to you. It's your fault." "You've got a seductive spirit. There's something wrong with you."

We got at the few things in Gloria's history that could in fact have been causing men to approach her wrongly, and things changed — but that didn't stop Fred's rages. He was still after her as though she could hardly wait to be unfaithful. So we tracked out the roots in Fred's early life. His mother had been unfaithful to his father. He had been more than merely aware of her illicit lovers, he had often been deeply shamed as these men came to the home when his father was out of town. It was easy to see that until he forgave his mother, he would project onto his wife that she would do what his mother did. He forgave his mother. We reckoned as dead on the cross his patterns of expecting that the woman of his life would betray his trust and attract illicit lovers to her bed.

For a while Fred was free. When he would take Gloria out to dinner and men's heads would swivel, he was only proud that he possessed such a gloriously beautiful wife. But no one had ever taught him about the ongoing discipline every Christian must undergo upon receiving the Lord and His healing of the heart and mind. He thought his old ways of feeling and thinking were dead once for all and would never trouble him again.

Of course they were dead. But they remained in the ground of his heart and mind, dead but ever present. When the pressures of work and children came upon him, and he let his prayer life slip, the old feelings and thoughts arose again. Fred then made the mistake so common among Christians (and non-Christians alike) that it is one of the primary reasons this book is being written — *he believed his rekindled fleshly feelings and thoughts were what he actually felt and thought, and so began to wrestle with them again, thus giving power and life to those old dead things to which they had no right. He soon had his problems back again, full-blown!*

What actually had happened was merely that his old habitual ways of thinking and feeling had flicked back into action. But let's think about it for a moment. We have the heart and mind of Christ. Our old nature has died with Him on the cross, and He is now living His feelings and thoughts within us, for us, as us, "I have been crucified with Christ; and *it is no longer I who live, but Christ lives in me. . .*" (Gal. 2:20, italics mine).

Fred had wrestled those old feelings and ways of thinking to effective death on the cross. He had been living in new and honorable ways of feeling and thinking about his wife. Therefore those old ways of thinking and feeling which were coming back to haunt him had no true reality. They were simply habitual ways of thinking and feeling, not what he as a born-anew Christian really thought in the present at all, though they claimed to be.

Fred erroneously believed that because those old thoughts and feelings came into his mind and heart they must really be what he thought and felt. That belief gave them life and power they had no right to possess — and so he resurrected his once-dead flesh and had to struggle unnecessarily with his problems all over again, as though he had never been healed. *Our carnal mind and heart would rather plunge us into the depths of recurrent troubles than let go of its control of us and die.*

When Long-dead Thoughts and Feelings Return

The first lesson to be learned in the renewal of the mind is not to believe old carnal feelings and thoughts when they come back after prayers for healing. How many counselors have wanted to drill this lesson into their counselees' heads! Old long-dead feelings and thoughts *will* return. If we believe these thoughts and feelings are what we really feel or think, we will have our problems back again — because we have resurrected what was dead, and have given it power in our life again.

Please hear it, Body of Christ, you have the heart and mind of Christ. When the old returns, it is only an echo of the old self, only an old, practiced habitual way, sounding off again with no real intention or life behind it. It is not what you really feel or think — unless you believe it and give it life and power. *The purpose behind it is the desire of the old self to regain its mastery of you.*

Some may be having difficulty understanding or accepting one or both of the concepts that our feelings and thoughts have a life of their own and do not want to die, and that sometimes what we think and feel is not really what we think and feel. Let me give you an example which may bring these things down out of theory to simple reality for you.

A two-year-old boy was being raised by parents who had swallowed the unbiblical notion that children younger than four or five ought not to be disciplined. One day he threw a temper tantrum. His parents leaped to comfort him (they should simply have hauled him up short and corralled his rampaging emotions for him). This happened several times. Now the boy had learned a powerful tool — he knew how to make those great big giants jump!

From then on, whenever he wanted something, all he had to do was to throw a temper tantrum and his parents would give in to his wishes. After a while he no longer knew whether he was in fact angry or not. Family and friends could easily see what was going on, even if the parents couldn't.

That manipulative habit of producing anger to get whatever he wanted had developed a life of its own within him. He now thought his angers were real and honest, though everyone else, by then even his parents, could see that what he thought he was thinking and feeling was not at all what he really thought and felt.

So we see that in fact sometimes what we think and feel is not at all what we really think and feel. But you say that was just a childish thing, not something adults would do? Right there is the major point of this chapter; listen again to that most familiar Scripture nearly everyone can quote: "When I was a child, I used to speak as a child, *think as a child, reason as a child,; when I became a man, I did away with childish things"* (1 Cor. 13:11, italics mine).

Our practiced ways of thinking and feeling which resurrect after being slain on the cross are precisely that — the ways we used to think and reason as children. Under pressure, we tend to regress to the familiar ways of the past. They may not have worked, may indeed have been a prison, but at least they were familiar — and by falling back into them, we have reinstalled our carnal, old self in control — even if paradoxically that means being out of control in our emotions and thoughts!

The Discipline Every Born-Anew Christian Must Learn

The discipline every born-anew Christian must learn is how to recognize when he is resurrecting an old fallen practice, so as to haul it restfully back to the cross again. We are crucifying anew, daily, the *childish* ways of thinking and feeling which our carnal nature would use to regain the throne of our life. For this reason St. Paul wrote, "I die daily" (1 Cor. 15:31).

We are created in the image of God. God is free. We have free will and a life of our own. The same is true of whatever we create within our own nature. Our self has a life of its own. Our emotions have a life of their own. So too, our carnal mind has a life of its own. Neither our feelings nor our thoughts want to die or to let go of their control of us. Our carnal mind *refuses* to lie down and quit its rule over us just because we have invited the

Holy Spirit to take charge of us. "For the mind that is set on the flesh is hostile to God; *it does not submit to God's law, indeed it cannot*" (Rom. 8:7 RSV, italics mine). Notice that this verse clearly says that our minds do have a life of their own — a life involving will, desire and intention. The carnal mind is "hostile," "does not submit." And remember — that chapter from Romans was addressed to born-anew Christians!

The Dislodging of the Carnal Mind

The rule of the carnal mind begins to be dislodged when we receive the Lord Jesus Christ as our personal Lord and Savior, and when we read the Word of God, pray, receive truth when confronted by brothers and sisters in Christ, minister to others in the Spirit, choose sound thinking in Christ, and so forth. Therefore our carnal mind fights back. It seeks any pretext to break out against sound judgment (Prov. 18:1, RSV). It casts up seemingly wise thoughts, objections and skepticisms, trying to involve us in unnecessary reasonings, clever sophistries and "foolish speculations" (2 Tim. 2:23). "It isn't logical to believe that." "You aren't making sense." "You have no business trying to help anyone else, you're a mess yourself." Anything will do — any thought, any seeming contradiction which *must* be resolved, any feelings which *have* to be settled. The more brilliant create the most clever smoke screens.

Our mind demands intellectual integrity, a tight system with no loop-holes, no contradictions. But in actual fact our mind couldn't care two hills of beans whether everything is kosher or not. It only wants to keep the Holy Spirit from becoming seated as the ruler of our hearts and minds. Who has not noticed that it is often the most brilliant who are the last to receive the gift of the Spirit? Or the gift of speaking in tongues?

The Holy Spirit breaks through and you utter a few syllables in your new heavenly language, and what does your mind do? — "Cut that out. You're only making that up!" "You're making a fool of yourself!" "This is silly." Nothing dislodges the carnal mind and embarrasses it more than for us to start spouting words it can't understand or control! What our mind actually wants is to keep its mental game going so that it won't have to relinquish the throne of our life.

That old saying, "The child shall be the father of the man," means to me that *our spirit is to rule our mind.* When the Holy Spirit enters, He intends to rule our spirit. *Through our spirit, the Holy Spirit intends to govern our mind, and by our renewed mind, to corral and direct our passions.* That is God's plan, His order for our interior being. But from our infancy, we have installed our conscious, carnal mind in control of our flesh, to rationalize our desires, protect our feelings, think our thoughts, and plan our steps. Whereas the Scripture says, "The mind of man plans his way, *but the Lord directs his steps*" (Prov. 16:9, italics mine). Our mind relishes its importance, and does not readily succumb to its death and retirement from control.

It is our lack of trust in God which our carnal mind uses to retain its throne. We are afraid if we let go, the Holy Spirit won't really take charge, and we will run amok and embarrass ourselves!

Lack of Trust

Lack of trust began in the womb, when our spirit was first shocked at the smog of mankind's sin and uncleanness which seeped through our mother's body and nauseated our nascent spirit (see the first four chapters of *Healing the Wounded Spirit*). Having been created within the purity of God, having some kind of rudimentary recollection of His holiness, we were shattered by waves of mankind's sickness in sin, invading and destroying the clarity and beauty of our spirit.

If we could have made cognizant our spirit's cry from within the womb, it would have been, "Where are you, Lord? Why are you letting this happen to me? You sent me to do a job for you — and now I am getting all mixed up and messed up. It isn't fair!" Our spirit "knew" that Ephesians 2:10 was true of us before our brain was formed, "For we are His workmanship, created in Christ Jesus for good works, which God prepared beforehand that we should walk in them." Our cry would be, "I'm becoming all messed up in this stinking morass of sin, and now how am I going to be able to do what you sent me here to do?"

Our ability to trust His Lordship was lost even as we were formed in the womb! As adults we think, at deepest levels, "He wasn't there for me then. He won't be there for me now." (In truth He *was* there, with us, even in the womb — see Psalm 139 — but we lost the ability to grasp that with telling reality). Unless a special gift of God's grace enables, we can't trust that if we surrender our carnal control of ourselves, *He will rule* us in safety and in peace.

If parents (who represent God to our childish mind — see the chapter, "How We See God," in *The Transformation of the Inner Man)* fail to apply appropriate discipline to corral our rampaging emotions, we are even more unconsciously sure as adults that God won't be there for us if we let go control of ourselves to His Holy Spirit.

Many parents have failed to be as present to their children as the children have needed them to be, more and more frequently as our society has increasingly lost its bearings and family structures have disintegrated. Therefore, more and more people find it increasingly difficult to trust enough to let the Spirit govern their lives, even though they may invite Him to do so.

Betty came because panic gripped her whenever anyone in authority addressed her directly, or loud sounds in the night awoke her. It wasn't difficult to reveal to her that her loud and abusive father had only spoken to her when he wanted to shout at her for supposed failures around the house, and that he was apt to come home at any hour of the night, drunk and abusive. She could easily see the source of her fearfulness. It was not hard to induce her to forgive her father. We could then reckon as dead on the cross her built-in alarm and tension-producing system. She had simply conditioned herself to go into panic whenever anything reminded her of those early experiences. Prayer set her free. She confessed she was no longer afraid in my presence, or in the presence of her boss, or anyone else — and she had even been sleeping like a baby.

But one day someone in authority spoke crossly to her, and whereas for several weeks she had been rejoicing that she hadn't gone into panic attacks, this day she did. It threw her. She thought, "The prayers haven't worked after all, maybe they have only been like a veneer which has now peeled off." She reasoned it was our fault.

She had come to us before we learned not to release someone like her before training her how to handle such things. All she had needed was to say to herself, "That's not really who I am. I'm not that fearful creature anymore. That one died with Jesus. I don't have to let these feelings get to me. This is just that old habit kicking up. I'll just ignore those feelings and go on about my business."

Our old habitual ways of feeling act like a bully with a little girl. If he can tease and pester enough to get her feelings riled up, he'll keep it up until she is frazzled out of her wits. But if a girl learns to stand up to a bully, telling him he can't bother her and is only making a fool of himself, and then ignores him, pretty soon he grows weary of the fruitless game and goes away. Had Betty responded in that manner, her feelings would soon have subsided. They weren't truly her feelings. She was a new creature in Christ, with all the courage and strength of Jesus inside her (see Phil. 4:10-13). But when she believed that because she felt that same old fear, it must be real, she let her feelings bully her right back into the same old series of panic attacks.

The Most Difficult Thing for Christians to Learn

Perhaps the most difficult thing for Christians to learn is that the fact that they feel or think something doesn't mean that they really feel or think that thing. Parents soon learn to discern when a child cries out from bed, "I'm thirsty," that sometimes he actually is — but most of the time he only thinks he's thirsty because he has learned that's one way he can get some attention and prevent himself from going to sleep.

To the child, it can be very real. He has convinced himself he's really thirsty. What we feel or think may have no more reality than a child's practiced habit of fooling himself at bedtime. It's that simple. Our old pre-Christian way of feeling or thinking kicks back into action, and we don't realize that it has no more reality than a child's manipulative cry in the night!

Stan had multiple angers which often cost him jobs and now threatened to undo his marriage. Together we dealt with the roots. It doesn't matter what they were; angers can result from frustrations with parents, suppressed angers at members of the family, birth traumas, playground experiences, whatever. The point is that in his case they had become an habitual way of feeling and expressing. We brought them to death on the cross.

For a while Stan was free. But when angers began to return, he was so upset that they had returned that that very fact increased his explosions worse than before! He too had not learned not to believe his feelings. *Our feelings and thoughts have such a life of their own within us that they are fully capable of waiting until just the right moment to flare back to life, so that we will take them up and adopt them again* — without the aid of the devil, though whenever he is around, you can bet he is delighted to take advantage of our naivete to get us going again.

When feelings and thoughts recur, and they surely will, in all of us, then it is that if we do not know what I've been teaching here, we can be grabbed by fear that we weren't healed after all! Beneath our built-in untrust of God is fear that our faith won't prove to have worked after all. So when the old way acts up again, that proves to our doubting mind what we always thought all along — it doesn't work! Our carnal mind uses that fear and lack of faith to retain its hold over us.

For this reason St. Paul wrote:

> Since then the children share in flesh and blood, He Himself likewise also partook of the same, that through death He might render power-less him who had the power of death, that is, the devil; *and might deliver those who through fear*

of death were subject to slavery all their lives."
(Heb. 2:14-15, italics mine)

The greater death we fear is not the physical. For most of us that death would be a hallelujah — we'd get to go home to the Father! What we fear most is death to our self, to our control of our own lives. For that reason we are kept in the lifelong bondage of our childish ways.

Jo Black had learned how to defeat herself. Remember how often the Holy Spirit said through John in Revelation, "To him who overcomes, I will give..."? (Rev. 2:7, 2:17, 2:26, 3:5, 3:12, 3:21). Overcomes what? His own recurring, self-resurrecting dead nature! (This is the same Jo Black whose story is told in "The Captive Spirit" in *Healing the Wounded Spirit*. All other stories in this book have been changed to protect confidentiality. We have her permission to tell her story as is, using her rightful name.)

Jo had been molested as a child. She had learned to defeat the man by turning off, dead to all natural responses. Though she was (and still is) a gloriously beautiful woman, she would just as soon Frank didn't bother her sexually. Marital sex contained no glory for her. It was just a duty to be endured. She could feel nothing good during it. And she felt horribly guilty for what she was doing to Frank, who was a good and kindly man, and a considerate lover. Then she was converted and filled with the Spirit. Many things changed overnight, but her sexual problems remained untouched. She still couldn't feel anything good during sex, though her new-found faith told her she should.

We uncovered the molestation. She forgave the man. And we hauled to death on the cross that practiced pattern of turning off to defeat the man. But the next several times when Frank approached her, she found rising in her the same old habitual thoughts and feelings, threatening to shut her down and plunge them into frustration again. By then, however, we had learned to train her in how to handle such things.

She merely recognized them for what they were — old dead things trying to regain life. And she said within herself, "That's not who I am any more. I don't choose those feelings. I choose to be open to Frank, and to feel good things in his embrace." After a little persistent effort, she broke through into a glorious time with Frank. Ever since then, they have enjoyed their sexual life more every year.

The tragedy is that so many Christians have never been taught the simple lessons of this chapter. They have never understood the continuing battle to subdue their own minds and feelings. So they plunge needlessly back into their ancient troubles, and seem to have no recourse but to blame and shout at the devil. He may use whatever handles we give him, but he is not the primary problem. Our own lack of understanding and discipline is what destroys us in these cases.

Sometimes a phrase from Revelation rings in my head: "And I saw one of his heads as if it had been slain, *and his fatal wound was healed"* (13:3a, italics mine). Of course that text is talking about a beast who is something altogether else than our subject, but it grabs me as a figurative or *rhema* word. Our carnal mind is surely a beast that received a mortal wound when we received Jesus as Lord and Savior! Note that it was a "head" that was slain. And the head was healed — it came back to life. *Our problem is to keep the beast of our carnal mind dead; it keeps coming back to life!*

The solution is easy. Just recognize its games. You don't have to struggle with its thoughts and resurrected old feelings all over again. Just do what Jo did. Merely relax, and say to yourself, "That's not what I really feel or think. I don't have to wrestle with that or give it any power. I choose (whatever new feelings and thoughts are appropriate in Christ). That's who I really am. I'll ignore these feelings and thoughts until they go away." "Lord, I choose your way, and I banish these old things from my heart and mind."

Don't get in a sweat trying to make it happen all at once. Your mind and feelings would love to continue tossing up junk, just to get you involved in struggling and striving. Pay those old feelings and thoughts no mind. You don't have to act on them just because they came into your head and heart. They have no real life unless you give it to them. Rest, and enjoy your new life in Christ!

2

Comprehending the
Way the Lord Heals

For God hath not given us the spirit of fear;
but of power, and of love, *and of a sound mind.*
(2 Tim. 1:7, KJV, italics mine)

He presented another parable to them,
saying, "The kingdom of heaven may be compared
to a man who sowed good seed in his field. But
while men were sleeping, his enemy came and
sowed tares also among the wheat, and went away.
But when the wheat sprang up and bore grain,
then the tares became evident also. And the slaves
of the landowner came and said to him, 'Sir, did
you not sow good seed in your field? How then
does it have tares?' And he said to them, 'An
enemy has done this!' And the slaves said to him,
'Do you want us, then, to go and gather them up?'
But he said, *"No; lest while you are gathering up
the tares, you may root up the wheat with them.
Allow both to grow together until the harvest;* and
in the time of the harvest I will say to the reapers,
'First gather up the tares and bind them in bundles
to burn them up; but gather the wheat into my
barn.' " (Matt. 13:24-30, italics mine)

Perhaps a word of balance to the first chapter
should be added here. There are occasions when
what we think and feel *is* actually what we *are*
thinking and feeling. Probably that happens so

much more often than what we were speaking of in the first chapter that fake feelings and thoughts are the exception rather than the rule. So, how are we to know the difference?

Discerning the Difference Between True and False Feelings

We cannot simply ignore, as having no reality, whatever we have not yet brought to effective death on the cross. *Whatever we feel or think, which Jesus would not entertain as His, is a signal to us that we need to track that thing to its roots and bring it to death on the cross.*

But if we have already wrestled an old way to the cross, its reappearance is no more than the self, trying to regain the throne of control within us.

Whatever has not found its way to the cross has tremendous impact when we think it or feel it. It's sweaty business. It grabs hold of us. But after a while, Christians who learn this lesson begin to discern when old dead feelings and thoughts pop up, that those areas aren't gripping them like they used to — unless they choose to believe them and give them reality and power.

Those old feelings and thoughts are more like flotsam and jetsam floating in the sea of awareness, whereas, before they died on the cross, they were like a powerfully erupting volcano demanding attention! If a Christian will just stop a moment, and reflect on what he is thinking and feeling, it will become progressively easier to discern what has reality and what doesn't, simply by the lack of driving power in the old habitual way.

It is necessary to learn this distinction, because *the way the Lord heals ensures that old feelings and thoughts will crop up again and again as we grow in Him!* In the last chapter, we spoke of old ways recurring some time after our healing — but the impression could have been taken that it only happens once or twice, and then no more. Nothing could be further from the truth. Old ways can and do rebound to life *countless* times and ways, for years and years — though they do become progressively easier to detect and defeat.

Dealing With the Roots

In the parable quoted at the beginning of this chapter, Jesus said to leave the tares in place, lest you uproot the good with the bad. In Matthew 3:10, John the Baptist said that the axe is even now being laid to the roots of the trees. But when a tree is cut down, seldom do men go to the trouble required to dig out all its root systems. Instead, they leave the roots in place in the ground.

For this reason St. Paul wrote, "See to it that no one comes short of the grace of God; that no root of bitterness *springing up* causes trouble, and by it many be defiled" (Heb. 12:15, italics mine). Note, the tree was dead. Those old ways of acting and feeling had truly died. But their roots (as in verse 15 above) had been left there, in the soil of our life, fully capable of "springing up" to cause trouble again.

Why? Why didn't He jerk them out once for all, and be done with it? Because God in His wisdom knew we have to be forced to stay close to Him in devotion. If He were to remove our problematic nature altogether and replace it with something Christ-like, our confidence would be in ourselves. We would soon succumb to the greater sin of pride. And we would quickly drift away from dependence on Him, thinking, "I can do it myself."

But by leaving our old practiced way there, intact inside us, dead but present, He installs an automatic thermometer of our distance from His fire of love. The moment we walk away from private devotions and/or from worship with others, our old nature begins to revive and we are driven back to our knees in prayer. So God leaves our sin nature intact within our roots.

Later, we'll show more reasons why God leaves our problems intact within us. For now, the point is that if we do not comprehend the way of our Lord's healing, two difficulties may arise.

The first is that we may wonder, "If I've still got them in my root system, capable of resurrection at any moment, what good did my healing do? Just what was accomplished through those prayers for healing?" In the story of Stan, in the last chapter, that was the depth of his fury. He was enraged that he had gone through all that soul-searching and prayer, seemingly to no lasting effect!

Before we face our old nature and die to it on the cross, *it has us*. We act impulsively and sometimes compulsively, blind-sided by forces

within us of which we have little or no awareness
— and we possess no power to overcome whatever
we are aware of! When we have repented, received
forgiveness and reckoned that aspect of our sinful
nature as dead on the cross, it can no longer control
us. We're aware of its con games. We catch our self-
delusions before they impel us into sinful actions.
We are no longer impelled into wrong decisions and
actions. We are free — so long as we remain humbly
dependent on Him at the foot of His cross.

*Our transformation is simply in our new-found
freedom to choose the way of Christ, and the power
by His Holy Spirit to live it, not something set in
concrete in ourselves, never again requiring
personal discipline and choice.*

The second thing which may assail us, if we
don't comprehend the way our Lord heals, is the
haunting fear that after all we may not have been
healed *at all.* Our carnal mind then uses that fear
to regain its hold on us. St. Paul wrote 2 Timothy
1:7 to counter that "... God hath *not* given us the
spirit of fear; but of power, and of love, and of a
sound mind" (KJV). The Revised Standard Version
puts it this way: "... but a spirit of power and love
and *self-control."* The New American Standard
Bible also translates this verse: "... power and
love, and *self-control."* And the New International
Version says, "... of power, of love and of *self-
discipline."* (Italics mine in each quote.)

What the King James Version translates as
a sound mind, all three modern versions render as
self-control and self-discipline! *When we cannot*

trust, overcome by a "spirit of timidity," or "fear"
(KJV), our carnal mind usurps the functions of the
renewed mind and maintains its own fleshly self-
discipline and control of us — or lack of control.

Our mind is one part of our soul. God has no
other plan for our soul than to slay it and re-form
it in Christ. Our carnal mind must come to its death
on the cross if we are to find freedom to think and
feel in new ways. But many Christians have failed
to comprehend the radicalness of that death. Too
many still think in terms of "mending." Healing
still means to them that something got broken, so
let's fix it. But when the Lord heals our soul, He
doesn't merely fix it, like repairing a machine so
it will run again. In that sense, *there is no healing*
for the soul.

Psalm 23:3 does say, "He restores my soul,"
and Psalm 19:7 says, "The law of the Lord is
perfect, restoring the soul," but we must understand that all Christian "restoring" proceeds by
the work of the cross. God has only one answer for
sin. "The soul who sins will die" (Ezek. 18:4). Our
Lord Jesus has become that death for us. Therefore, for us, healing and restoration are the same
as crucifixion and rebirth, not mending. *That*
means that our carnal mind cannot be adjusted or
retaught, it can only be slain.

When Paula and I have heard of those who
have truly been helped by counsel and prayer
returning to their sinful ways sometime later, we
have grieved even as St. Peter lamented,

For if after they have escaped the defilements of the world by the knowledge of the Lord and Savior Jesus Christ, they are again entangled in them and are overcome, the last state has become worse for them than the first. For it would be better for them not to have known the way of righteousness, than having known it, to turn away from the holy commandment delivered to them. It has happened to them according to the true proverb, 'A dog returns to its own vomit,' and 'A sow, after washing, returns to wallowing in the mire.' (2 Pet. 2:20-28)

Seeing that happen, we have cried out to the Lord to explain to us more fully (than what we have shared so far), why did they fall? Or more to the point of our own cry, "How did we fail them? What didn't we do?" Or, "What did we do wrong?"

The Lord made us aware that the first cause is their failure to comprehend His way of transforming of which we have been speaking. He added that since they thought they had become something *in themselves*, these people had become filled with pride in their flesh and so needed humbling. "For if anyone thinks he is something when he is nothing, he deceives himself" (Gal. 6:3).

The second cause, He said, is pride and self-confidence in knowledge, "I've learned the hard way. Now that I know myself, I'll never do that again." They thought themselves protected by knowledge — which in a measure was true, but not when pride and reliance upon self-knowledge supplant the Holy Spirit. The Trinity is not "Father, Son and Knowledge." It is only the Holy

Spirit, not knowledge, who keeps us walking uprightly in Him.

"Knowledge makes arrogant, but love edifies. If anyone supposes that he knows anything, he has not yet known as he ought to know" (1 Cor. 8:1b-2). *Pride of intellect had managed to reinstall the carnal mind as king of their lives.* Self, rather than Jesus, had again become the master. God *had* to humble them. "For all who are being led by the Spirit of God, these are sons of God" (Rom. 8:14).

It was humbling to realize that we had connected them more with knowledge than with our wonderful Lord Jesus Christ! The Scriptures say, "The purposes of a man's heart are deep waters, but a man of understanding draws them out" (Prov. 20:5, NIV). It is the task of Christian counselors to "look at the heart," ". . . for God sees not as a man sees, for man looks at the outward appearance, but *the Lord looks at the heart*" (1 Sam 16:7b, italics mine). We are like detectives, searching for the real "who-done-its" in the depths of the human heart. The search to track out the real roots of problems can become so enticing that unwittingly we entrap ourselves and our counselees in gnosticism — the fallacy of being saved by knowledge rather than the person of Jesus Christ! *When that happens, our carnal minds have again found a way to install themselves in control, in us and in our counselees.*

Moment-by-Moment Abiding in Jesus

The only antidote we know to the carnal mind's desire to control is to abide moment-by-moment in our Lord through prayer so that however incisive the insights by which the Lord sets him free, the counselee knows it happened by His grace and not first by keys of knowledge. *The love of our Lord must so overwhelm the counseling sessions and our prayers that both we who counsel and all who receive our counsel cannot help but know and celebrate that it was the wonderful presence and grace of our Lord Jesus Christ that did the work.*

It also helps to keep things as simple as possible. *The more clever and involved our diagnosis and our prayers, to that degree the more opportunity exists for the mind to reinstate itself as the champion of our salvation.* Avoid complexity. Remember that our Lord refused after a while to teach by any other means than by stories and parables (Matt. 13:34). Could it possibly have been partly because He had become determined not to let the minds of His disciples grab center stage?

We repented and prayed, "Lord, let your love so overwhelm us that whatever clues we discover in people's hearts, they know themselves to have been loved to life only by you."

Turning Away

The third cause our Lord revealed is simply the habit of turning away. Detaching our root systems from nurture in Him inevitably re-attaches us to our carnal roots and resurrects the carnal mind to rule our "tree of flesh."

Holy Fear

In this chapter, *the lesson we must learn in renewing the mind is to develop holy fear of its power to reestablish its kingdom.* "Christ was faithful as a Son over His house whose house we are, *if we hold fast our confidence and the boast of our hope firm until the end"* (Heb. 3:6, italics mine) — confidence in *His* faithfulness, not confidence in ourselves. We must come to see our carnal mind as our enemy, not our friend. We must gain a healthy respect for its cleverness, a holy fear of its ability to seduce us again and again.

On the one hand, our Lord wants us to rest confidently in Him. And on the other, we need to retain holy fear for our salvation's sake. May I suggest that our confidence should be unshakable in His love for us, in certainty beyond a shadow of doubt that our salvation is *guaranteed in heaven,* that we are permanently sealed in Him (Eph. 4:30). But as to whether we will come into the fulness of the abundant life He has for us *here on earth,* we need to cherish the fear that keeps us pressing into Jesus, calling for repentance and change.

Because we exist so much by thinking, and perforce use our minds to do that thinking, I know of nothing more insidiously persistent at slipping back into wrongful prominence in our lives than our own carnal minds! "The fear of the Lord is the beginning of wisdom, and the knowledge of the Holy One is understanding" (Prov. 9:10). And a little holy fear of our own mind's ability to deceive us might just be a part of that beginning of wisdom as well.

3

Developing Mental Disciplines and Habits of Constant Prayer

Pray without ceasing. (1 Thess. 5:17)

> *For those who are according to the flesh set their minds on the things of the flesh, but those who who are according to the Spirit, the things of the Spirit. For the mind set on the flesh is death, but the mind set on the Spirit is life and peace, because the mind set on the flesh is hostile toward God, for it does not subject itself to the law of God; for it is not even able to do so; and those who are in the flesh cannot please God. (Rom. 8:5-8)*

The first lesson of this chapter is prayer, constantly and continuously. I studied in Drury College, Springfield, Missouri, one of the finest liberal arts colleges of its day. Then I went to Chicago Theological Seminary, known then as the mecca of liberalism, modernism and intellectualism. Like Daniel and his three companions (Dan. 1:4-5), who were instructed in all the "... literature and language of the Chaldeans ... educated for three years," and like St. Paul, trained at the feet of Gamaliel (Acts 22:3), I had received the best the world had to offer!

But when I received the Lord Jesus Christ as my personal Lord and Savior, by revelation I saw the seductiveness of the worldly knowledges I had acquired (Col. 2:8), and I declared, "Lord, I don't want *my* mind. I want *your* mind. I believe I have your mind within me. *Let your mind live and rule all my thinking and feeling.* I don't want my knowledge. I want your truth. Purge my mind according to your Word. Take me on a never-ending Emmaus walk, and open your Word to me daily, upsetting and replacing whatever I have learned in the world. Bring my mind to death in all its knowledges and ways of thinking and ways of controlling my feelings, in all the ways I have learned to think and feel in the world."

I found it was necessary to say that prayer many times, and I renew it every once in a while. The Lord heard it the first time. I have to say it again and again so that everything in me hears it anew each time.

The Importance of Prayer

We have found that many Christians have somehow just assumed that once they were born anew, their minds must be okay. Nothing could be further from the truth! Very many have never said the kind of mental "sinner's prayer" I've outlined above. I strongly urge the reader to take time right now to make that prayer your own. Say it in your own way, or make up your own prayer, but do it! You'll have to come back to it many times, but you'll begin to find revelations breaking through like never before!

Our gracious Lord waits eagerly for the opportunity to take each of us on our own personal Emmaus walk so that He can open to us the things in the Scriptures concerning himself (Luke 24:27). It is our "traditions which make void the Word of God" (Matt. 15:2-6, Mark. 7:5-13). All of us possess countless traditional ways of thinking we have assumed are Christian but may not be at all.

When I began to say that prayer, the Lord began to open to me the wondrous revelations out of which have come our books and our ministry for Him. But the prayers did not end the war, they began it! Years later a great saint of the Lord prayed over me, "Lord, we thank you for the keen mind you have given John. We thank you for all its labors in accumulating knowledge. But now, Lord, it exaggerates its task and does too much. Still John's mind, Lord! Quiet it. Take it off center stage so that the Holy Spirit can rule it through John's spirit. Turn his mind down for a while, Lord. It won't lose power. He won't become dumb or stupid. After a while it will have more power than ever before, but then it will be ruled only by your mind, not his. It will be your servant, ruled by you, no longer the master but the slave."

That prayer brought great relief to me. My questions and doubtings abated. Mental distractions possessed less ability to interrupt my prayer times and sermon preparations. It became easier to recognize the anointing of the Holy Spirit and stay within its leadings. Discernment was no longer confused by picayune questionings. Revelations of insight and knowledge came much more frequently and easily. My ability to catch my carnal mind in its smoke screens and deceptions increased until it became fun — and the carnal mind tired of sending up flak!

I strongly urge the reader to pray that prayer also, hauling the unregenerate mind to its effective death on the cross. This also may have to be done many times. Our pesky minds have to be made sure we mean it! It would be better to have someone else pray that prayer for you.

Our mind naturally responds to authority and will recognize and obey the authority of the Lord when spoken through another much more readily than through ourselves. Otherwise, it says to itself, "Well, I'll wait awhile. Maybe he'll change his mind." It can't get away with that game when another voices the prayer — besides, the greatest problem of our minds is pride, and when others pray for us, that humbles us and helps to set the mind aside so that the Spirit can rule.

The Role of Discipline

The second lesson of this chapter is discipline, self-discipline in the Holy Spirit.

Those prayers must be followed by a *discipline of constant flash prayers.* The Christian life is not a matter of feelings. It is a matter of continual choices, of millisecond choosings within the stresses of living. Abiding in Christ demands moment-by-moment choices to live by His Word and by His example.

Early on, the Lord began to set the parameters for my mind and heart: first, the laws of God, boundaries I could not pass. And then He impressed on Paula and me that we were to check every thought before we accepted it, every feeling before we embraced it (and gave it life within us), every action before we did it, by some simple questions.

If thoughts were forming, "Is this the way Jesus would think?" If emotions were rising, "Is this what Jesus would feel?" If actions seemed to be prompted, "Is this what Jesus would do?" There was always to be only one answer, "If Jesus wouldn't think it or feel it or do it, neither will I."

Put the positive way, it was, "I *will* think and feel and do what Jesus would." We soon discovered that it was relatively easy, if we happened to be abiding in Jesus, not to think, feel or do what He wouldn't. But it was much tougher to do the positive thing. We found that we could more often stop ourselves from doing all three wrongly than we could make ourselves do the loving and considerate thing! *The discipline of trying to live positively like Christ is what brings us to our knees and to death of ourselves faster than anything else we have tried so far.*

Again, I suggest that the reader stop for a while to take time to pray that the Lord set that track into the deepest reaches of the heart and mind. "I will not think what you would not think, Lord Jesus. I will not let myself feel what you wouldn't allow in your emotions. I will not do what you wouldn't do."

I think you'll soon discover, if these prayers are a first for you, that they are somewhat like asking for the gift of patience! Like, say the prayer — and duck! Kidding aside, they'll set you on a path of adventure from which we hope you'll never recover!

I have forced myself (see Matt. 11:12) to live by that discipline until it has become somewhat automatic. I no longer have to think to remind myself. It pains me that my old self all too often reasserts itself; I'm still so often a stinker, and wish I could be as loving and kind as I see so many others being — but the difference is that now I can't get away with it! Automatically, that discipline catches me up short and brings me to repentance, and if I miss it, the Holy Spirit much more quickly and easily catches me, directly or through others.

Our mind ceases to be our enemy when we discipline it in Christ and give it good channels to run in. *If we do not pay the price of building such a discipline in prayer, we cannot defeat the fleshly rule of our minds.* In this regard, as in others, there are no instant-on saints. In this area, there can be no substitutes for our own efforts, no matter how much our Lord generously gives us through His grace. He has paid the price, once for all. But in His wisdom, He leaves some areas for us to conquer with Him, in Him. And this is one of those areas in which He will not do everything for us with no corresponding discipline and effort on our part.

Some Christians remain immature. Paula and I have observed that they are always those who refuse the discipline of flash prayers and the constant daily habit of checking every feeling and thought and action by the example of Jesus.

For me, Galatians 2:20 and 5:24 (being crucified with Christ) happens most effectively and frequently by flash prayers, instantly, silently, before responding to people and circumstances. If I slip up and react before I can catch myself, prayers immediately after the event accomplish repentance and that same death of the mind and heart.

But some confess that they can't manage to pray that instantly right in the midst of a happening. Our son Loren is a most effective minister, who has confessed that he is not good at that kind of instantaneous praying. So he uses his *will* to stop his mind and feelings or actions and makes himself do what is Christ-like. Later on, when he can find time, he prays it through. Either way — whatever way anyone can collar his mind and feelings and actions sooner or later it is prayer which must be employed to nail our flesh to the cross, or the flesh will eventually conquer our walk in Christ.

The most important key for dethroning the carnal mind is prayer. Brother Lawrence prayed as he washed dishes. Mother Teresa, whose order of charity ministers every day around the world in more than 300 places, constantly prays as she scrubs a floor or rides a train.

The habit of prayer, not merely in flash prayers, must become the normal life-breath of every Christian. Jesus lives in our heart. Hebrews 7:25 tells us, "He always lives to make intercession. . . ." So what is He doing in our hearts? Praying! Interceding for others! *The only way we can abide in Him is to allow Him to live His life in us; and that means that the only way He can live His life in us, as us, for us, is if we are continually involved in intercessory prayer for others.*

Basketball players practice dribbling and passing until those actions become so automatic they don't have to think about them in the incessant rush of playing. It must be so, for sometimes actions on the court happen too fast for thought. In the same way, Christians need to practice "praying without ceasing" until they no longer have to remind themselves to pray, they just automatically do it.

Can anyone imagine a person suddenly involved in a professional basketball game who never had spent the required hours of practice dribbling and passing? "Help," he would cry, "quick, somebody teach me how!" But by then it would be too late. It can't be learned that fast. In the same way, there is no way to victorious living in Christ other than to set oneself to practice to pray, *before* the hectics of the game make it too late.

Prayer takes the ball out of the hands of our carnal mind. All of us have doubtless seen some pray absolutely carnally, out of nothing but their own minds. But the longer one practices praying, the more the carnal mind finds it increasingly difficult to maintain its rule — especially when our prayers are coupled with the disciplines above, which would translate here, "I will not pray whatever Jesus would not pray, neither in thought or feelings or what I ask Him to do."

However, many have said to us, "I can't think fast enough to pray on the spot in English (or whatever language is native to them). But I can pray in the Spirit, so that's what I do." They mean that they pray silently in tongues. Great!

The first purpose of the gift of tongues is to refresh us. We see this in Isaiah 28:12, "Here is rest, give rest to the weary, and here is repose." The antecedent to "here" is found in verse 11, "Indeed, He will speak to this people through stammering lips and a foreign tongue." We know verse 11 is about tongues because St. Paul quoted that verse in First Corinthians 14:21 while teaching about the gift of tongues.

The gift of tongues is for refreshment — we grow tired in prayer, trying to think what to say next, whereas we can pray on and on when we don't have to think about what we are saying. And when our emotions are on fire, stirring the carnal mind to justify its passions, praying in tongues is intended to bring us into rest.

The literal translation of the Greek words, "pray constantly," is "to come to rest." Prayer, in known or unknown tongues, stills our passions and gives our spirit opportunity to rule us so that our renewed mind, the mind of Christ within us, can rise to ascendancy and find right ways to answer.

One of the primary purposes of the gift of tongues is to dethrone the carnal mind. Nothing embarrasses and frustrates our carnal mind more than for us to be mouthing words it can't understand or control! Every time we pray in a tongue, we lessen the hold of our carnal mind over all that we think and do. We exercise our faith beyond our mind and strengthen our spirit to reign under the discipline of the Holy Spirit.

But that is also why too many Christians seldom pray in tongues. "Oh, it happened once a long time ago, but it's never happened again." What a tragic misunderstanding of the Scriptures! Our carnal mind finds hundreds of theological, quasi-biblical and other reasons not to pray in tongues — or simply distracts by "important" thoughts — because the carnal mind knows that if we pray in tongues often enough, its rule will be broken!

Who has not noticed that it is frequently the most logical and rationalistic people who profess to have little use for the gift of tongues? "Oh, I suppose it has some value for some people, but I've just never seen much good in it." (The inference is that if you were only as strong or smart in your faith as he, you wouldn't think you needed that gift much either.)

Maybe such a person has spoken in tongues once or twice to prove he has received the baptism of the Spirit, but hasn't ever done it since. He thinks it's something ecstatic that has to happen to him, his carnal mind having blocked out all the teachings that say the prophets' spirits are subject to the prophets (1 Cor. 14:32) and that we can speak in tongues whenever we want to. "I'd rather have the gift of knowledge, or wisdom" (as though having the one excluded the other! — do we see how deceitful the carnal mind can be, all the while trying to sound so logical and wise?). The truth is that these people's minds desperately throw up smoke screens, lest the Holy Spirit be allowed to dislodge their minds' carnal rule.

Where the Warfare Is

Anyone who has sat down to hold morning devotions has discovered where the warfare is. We can hardly meditate a moment or enter into the first words of prayer before our minds interrupt with something — anything! The more logical, important or obviously needful the better.

If we turn and wrestle with our mind, trying to get it to shut up, even better yet — our mind has distracted us from prayer, busied us, and kept itself on center stage. Successful people of prayer have learned to ignore whatever their minds interject, however seemingly important. They don't wrestle with the mind, talk to it, or pay it any heed at all. They go right on blessing and praising God and interceding.

The more we learn to concentrate to pray, the more we lessen the hold of our mind's carnality. It is this struggle to fight our way clear of the static and jamming of our own minds in prayer which also makes us ripe for repentance and change. There must be a ripeness. Ripeness means powerfully coming to see the frantic battle of the carnal mind to stay in control, and growing to hate virulently its tricks and deceptions. I am certain St. Paul must have gone through this same mental warfare:

> *Those who are according to the flesh set their minds on the things of the flesh,... the mind set on the flesh is death,... because the mind set on the flesh is hostile toward God;... does not subject itself... is not even able to do so. (Excerpts from Rom. 8:5-7)*

> *See to it that no one takes you captive through philosophy and empty deception.(Col. 2:8a)*

> *We have renounced disgraceful, underhanded ways; we refuse to practice cunning or to tamper with God's Word. (2 Cor. 4:2 RSV)*

> *Abhor what is evil. (Rom. 12:9b)*

It is difficult to see our own mind as evil. After all, it has been the tool by which we have lived all our life. It has so often warned us, or guided us successfully into good things. But any counselor who has sat for hours penetrating the deceptions of counselees' minds, batting down their distractions and clearing away their smoke screens, is well aware of the iniquity of the mind! The difficulty is for common lay Christians to acknowledge its sinfulness sufficiently to accomplish effective repentance.

Whoever struggles daily to move past the objections and interferences of his mind to learn to center in our Lord in prayer grows daily more disgusted with his mind. But if that isn't enough, read on to the next chapter.

4
Prayer Groups and Service

The first to plead his case seems just, Until another comes and examines him. (Prov. 18:17)

Iron sharpens iron, So one man sharpens another. (Prov. 27:17)

The way of a fool is right in his own eyes, But a wise man is he who listens to counsel. (Prov. 12:15)

For by wise guidance you will wage war, And in abundance of counselors there is victory. (Prov. 24:6)

Pride only breeds quarrels, But wisdom is found in those who take advice. (Prov. 13:10, NIV)

If the struggle to learn to pray is not enough to bring us to ripeness, the next best way I know, perhaps the only remaining avenue for those not given to prayer, is to become an active, regular member of a small Christian support group.

Receiving From Others

If the first step in dethroning the carnal mind is fear, and the second is prayer and discipline, *the third is counsel, in this case not formal counseling, but the continual, loving confrontations of brothers and sisters who love us too much to let us get by with our practiced deceits.* When our brothers and sisters in the faith, who know us well enough not to be fooled by our con games, confront us again and again, when they smash our deceptions, " . . . speaking the truth in love . . . " (Eph. 4:15), we begin to see the " . . . old self, which is being corrupted in accordance with the lusts of deceit, . . . " and we commence to become willing to " . . . be renewed in the spirit of your mind . . . " (Eph. 4:22-23). Group life is intended by our Lord to make us ripe for change.

Sometimes we fail to apply appropriate Scriptures to ourselves because we delimit words too much. We may see that word "lusts" and think it refers only to sexual passions. But the word here refers as aptly to the greediness of our mind for control of us as it does to anything sexual.

Our fleshly mind lusts after power to rule all our emotions and thoughts and actions. Notice that the next words of that text talk about the mind — to be " . . . renewed in the spirit of your *mind.*" So it is that we are being corrupted by the lusts of our mind. Since we live behind the screen of our own thoughts, we seldom can see without aid how our own thoughts are corrupting us. That is why we need to be deeply involved and exposed to the scrutiny of a group who loves us. They can see what we can't — how our mind seduces us into its own tight little circles.

The God of Niceness

Our group must meet often enough, with regularity, having permission to accost us with truth in love, if we are to see incisively enough to learn to hate our minds' deceptions. Unfortunately, many groups succumb to the god of niceness, until too few tell one another the truth any more. The carnal mind fights honesty, vulnerability, openness and corporateness even as it fights prayer. "Don't be so open; it's too risky. You'll get hurt." "You don't have to tell everything, you know." "They can't handle it." What's your business is your business. Don't go telling all your private things." "He ought to keep his nose out of my business." "You don't really like those people anyway. They keep hurting you." "You don't have to listen to them."

Years ago, in our small group, we had decided that we would become vulnerable and would allow anyone in the group to speak truth to us and minister to the depths of our hearts. I set out to do that. Soon the group pointed out that not only was I controlling how much, what about, and just how they would minister to me, each time I would subtly turn the ministry around until I was ministering to everyone else! Behind that was not merely fear to become vulnerable and an over-large dose of parental inversion, but a carnal mind cleverly masking its determination to protect its domain behind a facade of concern for others. My carnal mind shot up smoke screens, lest it be dethroned by truth.

The Price of Corporateness

Whoever would truly have the mind of Christ must pay the price of corporateness. The price is the pain and fear of openness, especially since people often make mistakes, and sometimes intend to hurt. The price is also the humility of *being formed* by others. "And coming to Him as to a living stone, rejected by men, but choice and precious in the sight of God, you also, as living stones, are *being built up* as a spiritual house for a holy priesthood, to offer up spiritual sacrifices acceptable to God through Jesus Christ" (1 Pet. 2:4-5, italics mine. Note the passive voice — not building ourselves, but *"being built up."*) Only if brothers and sisters are allowed, often enough, to shatter our petty world of thoughts, do we break free from our carnal mind's hold over us.

There is no other antidote to the pride and isolationism of our carnal mind than becoming determined to submit ourselves to the ministry of others, however faulty we may fear them to be. A brother pastor I loved consented to be prayed for in our ministerial fellowship. The pastors prayed under such anointing that I who knew him recognized that every word they said was right on, straight to the mark of his needs. When they had finished, my friend stood and said, "Brothers, I know you meant well, but I must be the arbiter of my own soul, and it seems to me you missed me, so I'll have to reject that prayer." My heart sank! Within a few months, that pastor became mentally ill! We must become willing to listen, else our carnal minds will weave webs which keep us ever in bondage.

Spiritual Service
Service is the final way I want to discuss for dethroning the carnal mind. "For whoever wishes

to save his life shall lose it, but whoever loses his life for My sake, he is the one who will save it" (Luke 9:24). The theme text of this book, Rom.12:2, was set in the context of Romans 12:1, "I urge you therefore, brethren, by the mercies of God, to present your bodies a living and holy sacrifice, acceptable to God, *which is your spiritual service of worship*" (italics mine).

Whoever sets out to serve the Lord in any capacity — as prophet, pastor, teacher, intercessor, whatever — soon discovers that his one-time friend is now his sometime enemy. Our fleshly mind frequently distracts more than it helps.

Any pastor or teacher who has set time aside to prepare a message has wrestled with straying, vagrant thoughts and inabilities to concentrate until sometimes all his time has been frittered away. The carnal mind knows that if we become heavily engaged in serving, anointing will take over and nudge the carnal mind off the throne. If we persist in serving, the carnal mind will eventually be starved out and replaced by the mind of Christ altogether.

The carnal mind senses its coming demise and hauls in every kind of disruption it can think of. Again, we defeat it best by ignoring it. If we turn to castigate ourselves for becoming distracted, the mind has won even while we repent; we were distracted from selfless serving.

Whoever sets out to counsel others soon becomes keenly aware of how their minds dodge truth and find silly rationalizations and excuses.

That awareness of sin in others then reflects like a mirror until we cannot help but face our own deceptions. Whoever sets out to heal, be it physical or inner healing, learns to hate how Satan's deceptions operate to rob people of their healings (John 10:10b).

Our friend leaves our presence, having received prayers which tore at the roots of rejection that caused fear and anxiety. Satan drops a dollop of fear into his heart, tempting him to believe the prayers didn't work. His carnal mind leaps to find reasons why the prayers "weren't right." "That counselor didn't really understand me." "Oh, I just don't have faith enough to make this work." "That stuff may work for others, but it sure doesn't work for me." And so the carnal mind gleefully dismantles the prayers for healing. One has to witness that process only a very few times to come to hate the carnal mind's interference! Laterally, that rapidly makes us aware of our own con games.

Learning to Love the Mind of Christ Within

The greatest effect of serving is that we learn to love the mind of Christ in us. As we serve, inspired by the Holy Spirit, we are often surprised and overjoyed at the wondrous insights our renewed mind uncovers. Practicing to serve thus builds into us Christ's way of thinking; it installs His mind upon the throne of our life — *if we remember "... do not be haughty in mind, Do not be wise in your own estimation"* (Rom. 12:16, italics mine). "For through the grace given to me I say to every man among you not to think more highly

of himself than he ought to think; but to think so
as to have sound judgment, as God has allotted to
each a measure of faith" (Rom. 12:3).

Section 2
The Depths
of the Problem

5
Deep Ruts

See to it that no one comes short of the grace of God; that no root of bitterness springing up causes trouble, and by it many be defiled. (Heb. 12:15)

And the axe is already laid at the root of the trees; every tree therefore that does not bear good fruit is cut down and thrown into the fire. (Matt. 3:10)

The question which cries for an answer is: "How shall our renewed minds find sufficient freedom from the flesh so as to set truly righteous directions for the heart to follow?" We have all heard bigoted Christians wrongly spouting Scriptures, unaware their minds were not yet renewed, still serving the foul passions of their hearts. Who has not grieved to see born-anew people warping Scriptures to suit decisions their renewed minds had little part in making? So the question is: "What holds the renewed mind on the track of the Lord's nature despite the storms and deceptions of the heart?" In the end, just what is it that enables our minds to choose His righteousness?

Finding Freedom From the Flesh

To me, there are at least two primary answers: One, we who are Christians must persistently

77

crucify the flesh daily so that the storms of our hearts are settled. Two, devotion and service in the Spirit must be so tender and full that a Christian can truly be "...diligent to present yourself approved to God as a workman *who does not need to be ashamed, handling accurately the word of truth"* (2 Tim. 2:15, italics mine).

Inner healing seems to be the obvious way to accomplish number one; and of course all inner healing does help to reduce the pressure of our deceptive heart's attempts to rule. But many have gone through a lot of inner healing and have not yet obtained much objectivity. *There remains a need to crucify the mind itself, in all its deepest ruts.*

What are "deep ruts?" There are two kinds. The first are tracks, thought-patterns in our minds which were *not trained into us,* nor chosen in experience, but which are part of us as "givens," inherited simply because we are descendants of Adam and Eve. The second are our ways of thinking *we built* into ourselves in infancy and early childhood, so deep we may not be aware they exist, though they guide us daily, and can entrap us.

There are also combinations of both inherited and developed ruts. *Deep mental ruts exist in all of us,* whether born-anew or not. All too often they serve as channels for rivers of fleshly passions to rise nearly unchecked into dominance and control. Deep mental ruts may be one of the primary reasons St. Paul commanded us not to be conformed to this world but rather to be transformed according to the Word of God!

When I was a boy, few paved roads existed outside of major highways. Rains made quagmires of most country roads. Vehicles soon carved deep ruts, sometimes for miles on end. A favorite joke was, "Choose your rut carefully; you'll be in it for seven miles!"

Our minds inherit and build the same kind of deep tracks. In those days, if a driver were not careful when ruts became too deep, the slightest bump could tear out the oil pan. Similarly, when the ruts of our minds run so deep that we lose our flexibility (can't turn out of them), the slightest bump in life threatens to tear out the "oil" of joy in the Spirit. Turning out of deep ruts in the mind requires the same kind of tough and careful "steering" that country driving did then. We accomplish it only by the grace of Jesus and the toughness of determination.

Henry came to the Lord in a burst of deep emotion. He loved Jesus with every part of him he could command. But Henry had spent years developing ways of thinking about and obtaining money; and ways of thinking about taking revenge whenever anybody stepped on his favorite projects or hurt his friends. When he became a member of the trustees' board of the church, try as he would, there was no way he could get his mind to wrap around and embrace concepts of faithful giving to others. He kept thinking in "businessmen's hard-headed terms," and demanding that the rest of the board think "as practically" as he did. His mind ran in that kind of a rut, no matter how hard he tried to understand men of faith. (What pastor has not struggled with that mental rut in the members of his church?!)

When a young lad took advantage of his daughter, Henry was put squarely on a pinnacle of sweaty choices! His new-found faith told him that he should forgive. The love of Jesus welled up within him, prompting him to open his arms and embrace his wounded daughter and her frightened friend. But his will jerked around in the deep ruts of his mind. It took a tremendous miracle of the Lord's own personal touch to break Henry out of the grip of his mind.

A friend grew up in a very liberal church, in which dignity and privateness of conscience were burned into the depths of members' minds and hearts. Our ministerial alliance brought in an evangelist from South Africa for a county-wide series of evangelistic meetings. One night I happened to be standing across the aisle from my friend while the evangelist was giving the altar call and the power of the Holy Spirit was falling like a downpour over the congregation.

My friend had already been struggling, before the meetings, just to make himself decide to come to such a thing, where public displays of emotion might happen and people might be induced to say things that might be very private and embarrassing. He didn't believe in that sort of thing —

"religion ought to be private" — "no side-show-of-emotion kind of thing!"

My friend stood at the aisle, one foot halfway out, physically swaying back and forth, as he wrestled with the conviction of the Holy Spirit. I knew this was his moment before God, and I began praying — fervently. The Holy Spirit had run smack up aganst the deep mental ruts of his upbringing, and the interior battle within his mind was fierce. It broke my heart that his carnal mind won that battle — he sat down — and I saw, with equally fierce determination to destroy it, the enemy of his spirit — his deep mental ruts, holding him captive when his spirit knew which way he should go. I have hated mental ruts with utter passion since those days.

Deep Ruts — Deep Roots

Deep ruts are also often the mental shape of *deep roots* within us. What are roots? *Roots are practiced hidden ways of drinking nurture and fulfillment from God, from others, self and nature.* A root is an habitual manner of receiving. It is a system for getting, not for giving. A root is a way our inner being has developed to obtain whatever it deems is necessary for survival and well-being.

Roots are hidden in the same way that we as tiny children built ways of walking and talking until they became automatic systems requiring no continued, conscious effort. That is God's economy. If we had to concentrate on how to walk and talk, we would wear ourselves out trying to do the simplest functions. If we had learned to walk in Texas, we might have built an unconscious habit of walking with a long, free-swinging step. If in Japan, with quick, determined steps. If we had learned our speech patterns in Georgia, we might say with a drawl, "Y'all come back now, y'heah?" In Connecticut, we might speak of our "daag" having leaped over a "laag" to get into our neighbor's "pahty" — of all things for him to be "theah!" The very "idear!"

We drawl or clip our speech because that was built in by the time we were six. Those formations happened so long ago we have forgotten or never really knew we learned them. Thus our practiced ways are hidden to us. Only when we become exposed to others do we see that our way is not always everyone else's.

It takes great effort to change roots and/or deep ruts. For instance, we may succeed in overcoming accents, only to flash back to childhood patterns of speech in moments of excitement. Akin to that, emotional and behavioral roots and mental ruts remain hidden and often reassert themselves whenever passion overcomes.

The analogy is misleading in one respect, however. Walking and talking are things *within ourselves,* ways of moving and expressing. But roots are ways of reaching *beyond ourselves* to drink from others what we need. Roots are the practiced and long-forgotten ways we automatically receive nurture from all around us. Roots of a tree reach into the earth to send water and nutrients racing through cambium cells into every branch and leaf. Just so, through our root systems, our spirit reaches to God, others, our own inner wells and nature to drink affection, acceptance, love, approval, embrace, etc. — or, unfortunately, to feed on rejection, refusal, criticism, bitterness and aloofness, etc!

Some root systems are part of us because of Adam and Eve, as we will see shortly. Other systems we established in the very first experiences of life. Even from within the womb, our spirit is keenly sensitive. It reaches to our mother and father and senses invitation, welcome and embrace — or rejection. *Our spirit has built its first tap roots long before our birth.* (For further information, see the first four chapters of *Healing the Wounded Spirit).*

Experience with parents, siblings and others confirms, or upsets and rebuilds, both the root systems we inherit and those we originate. By the time we are six, both kinds of roots are firmly established. From then on, until about twelve, we are busy building and establishing the strong trunk of character on which the limbs and leaves of our personality will depend for the remainder of our lives.

Deep ruts, as part of our root system, either bless, inhibit, or prevent altogether our reception of nurture. There *are* good roots and ruts. Even these need to find their death on the cross, lest our righteousness be of the flesh rather than the Holy

Spirit. But throughout these chapters, we will speak only of bad roots and ruts.

Roots are what our *spirit* uses to drink nurture; *deep ruts* are the *mental shape* of those roots. For example, if an infant receives little cuddling but much harsh discipline, his spirit can be crippled in its ability to drink nurture, and his mind most likely will have accrued built-in thoughts about what authority figures and loved ones will do. That way of thinking may strangle whatever good roots remain. Deep ruts may cause him not to notice touches of love in adulthood, or may twist true touches of love into paranoid notions of neglect or abuse. Long after his conversion, years after his conscious mind has received the saving love of Jesus and acknowledged with delightful surprise the thousandfold loving embraces of spouse and children and friends, his deep mind may still wallow in ruts of misconceptions and self-pity.

Deep ruts reside in the heart. Truly, "... *for out of the heart come evil thoughts*" (Matt. 15:18).

Inherited Roots

Root systems inherited from Adam and Eve are *common to all;* no one has escaped having them. We share equally in original sin; no one has received unique dosages. What we *do* with inherited roots *is* unique.

In primary school we learned that fractions have common denominators and multiple numerators. So it is with roots. Inherited roots are like denominators, common to all. How they are starved or developed, remain single and simple or become combined and complex, wax weak or powerful, are consciously recognized or become unconscious drivers, is like numerators, varied and diverse, unique to each person's history.

Roots and deep ruts in all of us are so strongly established and so stubbornly persistent in functioning the way we first inherited or constructed them that that fact alone is a foremost need to renew our minds — and a major reason for the continued pain of sanctification and transformation long after we receive our Lord Jesus as our Lord and Savior.

Years ago the Sunshine Silver Mine at Kellogg, Idaho, sustained the most unlikely thing ever to happen in a hard-rock mine — a wood fire! Wooden support beams and rail ties, which had become soaked with oil, smouldered and burned. That sent carbon monoxide throughout all the stopes. Ninety-one men died. Medical rescue teams said to our ministerial group, "Human blood is so foolish it will accept carbon monoxide three hundred times to one over oxygen!" That was what caused the ninety-one to die. Though plenty of oxygen had been present within the smoke, their blood had chosen death-dealing monoxide rather than life-giving oxygen!

In the same way, once our roots have learned to seek and feed on rejection, hatred, criticism, etc., though plenty of love and encouragement, affection and approval may abound, our root system may pick out that which brings misery and death rather than life. Three hundred people may compliment and affirm us, but if one alone criticizes, we can become horribly upset!

Fortunately, our root system operates less stupidly than the blood in those ninety-one. It does not always choose death 300 to one! We do receive some nurture. Nevertheless, all too many people have so often unconsciously chosen to receive death and have mixed so much death into life as to remain emotionally crippled in the normal, "smoke-filled" nurture we must all dwell in. In most Christian homes, even in some without Christ, enough "oxygen" of love was present to have made life abundant and happy, but too often we have failed to be able to choose it. That is why renewal of the mind must continue, long after practices of behavior have found their effective death on the cross, lest our carnal minds re-attach to our sick roots and warp our choosing into sickness. For this reason St. Paul wrote, "Take care, brethren, lest there should be in any of you *an evil unbelieving heart,* in falling away from the living God" (Heb. 3:12, italics mine). As with ruts, it is in the heart that our roots live — *and cause us to choose wrongly.*

Notice that the Lord advised against removal of roots:

> *He presented another parable to them, saying, "The kingdom of heaven may be compared to a man who sowed good seed in his field. But while men were sleeping, his enemy came and sowed tares also among the wheat, and went away. But*

when the wheat sprang up and bore grain, then the tares became evident also. And the slaves of the landowner came and said to him, 'Sir, did you not sow good seed in your field? How then does it have tares?' And he said to them, 'An enemy has done this!' And the slaves said to him, 'Do you want us, then, to go and gather them up?' But he said, 'No; lest while you are gathering up the tares, you may uproot the wheat with them. Allow both to grow together until the harvest; and in the time of the harvest I will say to the reapers, 'First gather up the tares and bind them in bundles to burn them up; but gather the wheat into my barn.' " (Matt. 13:24-30)

Inner healing, therefore, never uproots a root. Faith builds strength the same way a muscle does, by continual exercise. The strong habit of depending on Him is made perfect by wrestling with roots of weakness. Thus, "My strength is made perfect in weakness" (2 Cor. 12:9, KJV). Prayer for inner healing slays the power of bad character sustained by bitter roots. It lays the axe (the sword of truth) to sin-filled root systems so that trees of bad character and consequent bad behavior are cut off from sustenance and power to act (Matt. 3:10). But the continued existence of death-seeking tap roots in the soil of our life ensures the continuance of fleshly weakness — which builds the muscle of faith by continued struggle!

That struggle is a battle to overcome the way we feel and subsequently think in our carnal minds. *When trees of character have been dealt a death blow and have been cut off from refreshment, it is fleshly feelings and consequent habitual wrong ways of thinking which re-attach dead trees to roots and resurrect bad behavior.* It is, therefore, imperative to learn to renew the mind so as not to be re-conformed to the world. We come into rest and enjoy abundant life in Christ when we build into ourselves disciplines of perceiving the seductive actions of bitter roots and ruts, and quickly and easily reckon them as dead on the cross (Rom. 6:11).

6

Inherited Roots and Consequent Ruts From Adam and Eve's Sins in the Garden of Eden

> Nevertheless death reigned from Adam until Moses, *even over those who had not sinned in the likeness of the offense of Adam,* who is a type of Him who was to come. (Rom. 5:14, italics mine)

> *For if by the transgression of the one, death reigned through the One,* much more those who receive the abundance of grace and the gift of righteousness will reign in life through the One, Jesus Christ. *So then as through one transgression there resulted condemnation to all men,* even so through one act of righteousness there resulted justification of life to all men. *For as through the one man's disobedience the many were made sinners,* even so through the obedience of the One the many will be made righteous. (Rom. 5:17-19)

Every human being possesses many deep spiritual tap roots as part of our heritage from Adam and Eve. Original sin is not merely legal descendancy from generation to generation (Deut. 5:9). Sin also descends through inherited roots, gene to gene, age to age. Already in the womb we know how to drink in rudimentary ways from God and from evil as instinctively as a newborn baby knows to suckle at its mother's breast. No one is needed to teach a baby to breathe or wet its diapers.

Likewise, our spirit instinctively looks to God. Within that instinct, because of Adamic sin, are root ways of alternately seeking and fleeing, loving and rebelling, accepting and rejecting, searching and hiding, wanting and not wanting, desiring God and choosing instead "messes of pottage."

As Augustine said, "We were created *in* God and we are *restless* until we return to Him." Countless ambivalent patterns inhabit us as part of the package of being human in the track of Adam and Eve. We do not have to invite them, seek them, or choose them. *Root rituals and deep ruts of thought exist a priori; they are part of us before we learn or build anything ourselves.*

Original Sin

Let's make real the concept of original sin expressed in those familiar Scriptures quoted above. It seems to me that Christians often give lipservice to the idea of original sin without real comprehension. We need to see that St. Paul was not merely expounding a theory, or merely proving logically that we are sinners so that we will accept salvation. He was teaching about the devastating reality of our sin nature from age to age, person to person, willy-nilly. *We transform that understanding from theory to actuality in ourselves when we comprehend the fact of the reality and power of roots and deep ruts in our minds,* as we will show in the rest of these chapters.

But first, let us see that St. Paul also taught that we know God instinctively in our spirit and that that knowing is corrupted by sin:

> For the wrath of God is revealed from heaven against all ungodliness and unrighteousness of men, who suppress the truth in unrighteousness, because that which is known about God is evident within them; for God made it evident to them. *For since the creation of the world* His invisible attributes, His eternal power and divine nature, *have been clearly seen,* being understood through what has been made, so that they are without excuse. For even *though they knew God,* they did not honor him as God, or give thanks; *but they became futile in their speculations, and their foolish heart was darkened.* (Rom. 1:18-21, italics mine).

Let's look to the story as God tells it to see how and when our sinful roots began and how they function:

> Then the Lord God formed man of dust from the ground, and breathed into his nostrils the breath of life; and man became a living being. And the Lord God planted a garden toward the east, in Eden; and there he placed the man whom he had formed. And *out of the ground* the Lord God caused to grow every tree that is pleasing to the sight and good for food; the tree of life also *in the midst of the garden,* and the tree of the knowledge of good and evil. (Gen. 2:7-9, italics mine)

Observe that the writer of Genesis makes a distinction between those trees that grew "out of the ground," contrasted to "the Tree of Life" and "the tree of the knowledge of good and evil." It is not said that the latter two grew out of the ground.

These appear to offer a different kind of fruit than those which grew from the ground.

The Tree of Life

The Tree of Life appears throughout the Scriptures, from Genesis to Revelation, and so also does the symbolism of trees. In Psalm 1:3 the man who does not walk in the counsel of the wicked nor stand in the path of sinners ". . . will be like a tree firmly planted by streams of living water, which yields its fruit in its season, and its leaf does not wither." In Daniel 4, Nebuchadnezzar was frightened by a dream which none of his soothsayers had been able to interpret. But Daniel made it clear that the great tree of his dream referred to the king's own mind, which would be cut down because of pride, until ". . . you recognize that *it is* Heaven *that* rules" (v 26). I believe the symbol of the tree refers mainly to the "tree" of character within every person.

In the Garden of Eden, the Tree of Life is the Word who became our Lord Jesus Christ (John 1:14). Therefore the Tree of Life is His matchless character and graciousness, available as nurture for Adam and Eve. In us, since the Fall, some trees symbolize our evil character which the Lord must cut down, as in Matt. 3:10, ". . . the axe is already laid at the root of the trees; every tree therefore that does not bear good fruit is cut down and thrown into the fire."

The story of God and man, of heaven and earth, culminates in the vision of the great Tree of Life in Revelation 22:1,2:

> And he showed me a river of the water of life, clear as crystal, coming from the throne of God and of the Lamb, in the middle of its street. And on either side of the river was the tree of life, bearing twelve kinds of fruit, yielding its fruit every month; *and the leaves of the tree were for the healing of the nations.* (Italics mine.)

Here we see unmistakably that the Tree of Life is our Lord Jesus Christ, His character and the fruits of His nature. Moreover, we have become His "leaves" ". . . for the healing of the nations." The promise is that *His* character shall become *our* character; and He will heal others through us.

> Then the Lord God took the man and put him into the garden of Eden to cultivate it and keep it. And the Lord God commanded the man, saying, "From any tree of the garden you may eat freely; but from the tree of the knowledge of good and evil you shall not eat, for in the day you eat from it you shall surely die." Then the Lord God said, "It is not good for the man to be alone; I will make him a helper suitable for him." (Gen. 2:15-18)

Note, there was no proscription regarding the Tree of Life. Adam may eat freely of *any* tree in the garden *except* the tree of the knowledge of good and evil. This means that before sin prevented him, he was at liberty, even enjoined, to partake of the Tree of Life! Note also that eating of the tree of the knowledge of good and evil is disobedience, thus sin, and recall that *"The soul who sins will die"* (Ezek. 18:4, italics mine). Observe particularly that when the command was given, Eve had not yet been created!

In His wisdom, God has never let it be known whether Adam carefully told Eve, and she forgot, or whether he failed to tell her accurately — or at all. If he was like me, he probably forgot to tell her! In any case, she made some drastic mistakes.

The first mistake was that she talked with the serpent at all (lest we judge unfairly, let's remember that hindsight is cheap and we have the benefit of history's wisdom). The second was that apparently Eve visited with Satan and made her decision apart from Adam, or else he was silent — or perhaps her entire conversation with the devil was conducted mutely, within herself.

Genesis 3:6 says ". . . she gave also to her husband *with* her . . . ", so either he was present, or else he arrived at that moment. Again the wisdom of God does not answer whether Adam walked apart from Eve, or failed her, or she left his shelter. Whatever did in fact happen, *from that lack of cohesiveness and attention to one another comes the first of our inherited deep roots and ruts. Perhaps the most common problem we counselors deal with in marital counseling is that couples do not communicate properly.*

Before Roger Bannister ran the first sub-four-minute-mile, no one could break the four-minute barrier. Now, almost any competent miler can run the mile under four minutes! Forerunners set patterns, enabling others to follow. In the same way, *everything Adam and Eve did established the*

*tracks in which our spirits and minds and hearts
would run.*

Engrams in Our Nature

Worse, the sins of Adam and Eve acted like
engrams in our nature. An engram is *"A persistent
protoplasmic alteration* hypothesized to occur on
stimulation of living neural tissue *and to account
for memory.* Also called 'memory engram,' 'neuro-
gram' " (*Reader's Digest Illustrated Encyclopedic
Dictionary,* emphasis ours). Engrams are caused by
blows so traumatic they create patterns which our
motor reflexes and even our physical cells repeat
automatically from then on.

When I was in high school, I worked after-
hours and Saturdays for Joplin Furniture
Company. One day I was doing some painting next
to the linoleum department. A lady wanted to see
the pattern of a tightly rolled coil of linoleum,
standing on end near me. Wanting to be helpful but
having paint on my hands, unaware that the roll
weighed over 400 pounds, I attempted to lower it
to the floor while holding on to it with nothing but
my wrists. It toppled with a resounding crash onto
my right big toe, instantly pulverizing the tip of
the bone! Ever since then, that toe has produced
nothing but a yellowed, gnarled, ugly toenail.

That is what an engram is, a blow which
causes the body to set itself into unchanging
patterns. *In like manner, every action of Adam and
Eve set into our nature roots and ruts so deeply
and firmly established that only the cross of Christ*

can overcome them and enable us to change! That is how original sin affects us all in the present, through tendencies and stubborn practices set like engrams into our old nature, still effective long after we come to Jesus, until we bring them to death on the cross.

So it is that because Adam and Eve failed to communicate, you and I suffer the same tendency, the same mental rut. The "blow" of Adam and Eve's failure has stamped into us such an engram that every marital couple since then must struggle against the ruts of their flesh to keep the lines of communication open and flowing.

Herein lies the first and most important healing lesson of these chapters, for how shall we deal with that fact? Not merely by becoming determined to try harder, nor trying to remember always to talk things out. That may help, but it won't solve the problem.

Each root and each rut we discuss as we proceed through these chapters needs to be brought to the cross in prayer if we are to be set free in any lasting way. I know that we learn best by repetition, so I'll repeat this admonition again and again, hoping by that to build into us a new rut of thought and healing practice.

Satan, being the wily deceiver he is, began in the same manner door-to-door salesmen approach gullible housewives today. In order to encourage confidence in the flesh so that women will purchase without waiting to consult their husbands, salesmen ask a number of questions wives ought to be able to answer easily. So Satan asked Eve a question I'm sure he thought she would answer correctly. "Indeed, has God said, 'You shall not eat from *any* tree of the garden?'" (Gen. 3:1, italics mine). Not being omniscient, even Satan must have been surprised when she answered:

> From the fruit of the trees of the garden we may eat; but from the fruit of the tree *which is in the middle of the garden,* God has said, "You shall not eat from it *or touch it, lest you die!"* (Gen. 3:2b and 3, italics mine)

There had been no command not to touch. Eve added to God's command. That error has become instinctive, a deep rut of thought in all of us. How frequently we add to God's commands and so disgust ourselves with dry obedience! For example, many early Pentecostals added to God's Word about modesty of dress until dowdiness became tantamount to holiness (1 Pet. 3:1-6)! Make-up was forbidden. Dresses and sleeves had to be of prescribed lengths. Even moderate necklines were forbidden. Hair had to be done up just so. Missing the intent for simple modesty, they added rules and regulations until obedience became odious. The next generation filled our counseling offices as we struggled to keep them from rejecting the Church and sometimes the Lord as well!

From before Jesus' day till now, many of us tend to make the Sabbath day a prison instead of a rest. We add to God's Word concerning the Sabbath. And we have added such rules as: "Thou shalt not play cards," "Thou shalt not go to movies," "Thou shalt not dance." Good advice, considering what most of those things have become in these days — but these rules are not found in God's Word.

Psalm 19 informs us, "The law of the Lord is perfect, restoring the soul" (v 7), and "The precepts of the Lord are right, rejoicing the heart" (v 8a). Obedience to God's law should always be refreshing to us, were we free from the engram of original sin. If we are to become able to interpret God's Word rightly and so *enjoy obedience*, the remedy is simple. Not "I will make myself obey every jot and tittle of the law!" But "Lord, bring me to death in my practiced, hidden ways of reading your Law. Bring to death on the cross the mind I inherited from Adam and Eve, and renew in me the mind of Christ, so I may see as He saw and obey as He obeyed."

Eve made another, more drastic error. She said the tree whose fruit they were commanded not to eat was ". . . the tree which is in the *middle* of the garden . . ." (v 3a). But Genesis 2:9b says that it is the *Tree of Life* which is "in the *midst* of the garden . . ." Eve so confused the command that she didn't know which tree was actually the forbidden one! This means that she had not been feeding where she should, on the Lord Jesus Christ! She had been feeding everywhere else.

Because she had not been feeding on the Tree of Life, and thus was not being nurtured by the source of life who became our Lord Jesus Christ, her spirit had become weak and, therefore, vulnerable to delusion. From that error we inherit our root tendency to feed everywhere else than on Jesus! Who has not battled to keep his mind on track nearly every time he tries to have morning devotions? Who has not at some time struggled to stay awake while reading that most exciting book of all books, the Bible? Who has not found his mind wandering during intercessory prayers? Or while listening to good sermons? Or trying to plan next week's Sunday school lesson? Where did that troublesome rut come from? In Eve's wandering to everything other than the Tree of Life, of course. *That mistake set the mold for our minds to follow from then on.*

How can we get free from it? "Lord, crucify my habit of wandering everywhere else than to you. Teach my heart anew to center in you. Fasten my mind to feed on the Tree of Life who is my Lord Jesus Christ." We may have to say that prayer dozens of times before our mind takes hold of it in earnest.

A worse consequence of Eve's error was idolatry. When we do not put God at the center of life, something else *has* to fill that vacuum. Nature abhors a vacuum. We *will* fill the center of life with *something.* Thus Eve was ripe for temptation. Satan stepped in to fill her hunger for truth. *Just so, idolatry has become the most besetting sin of all mankind.*

Idolatry lies behind every other sin; for whatever we choose rather than God's command has become more important to us than God. Throughout the Old Testament, the constant theme of the prophets was to thunder against the idols to which Israel returned as regularly as night follows day.

Who among us today could withstand the charge that we worship the "boob tube"? Or prosperity? Or our own good life (the most common guise the god of Mammon wears today)? *It is a powerful rut within us all to make anything and everything rather than Jesus the center of life.* The answer? "Father God, lay the axe of truth to my mind's wandering ways. Center me anew and afresh in my Lord Jesus Christ."

(I suggest the reader take a moment to pray each of these prayers as we go through them paragraph by paragraph.)

A third consequence of that error is that Eve inadvertently placed Satan at the center of her life. When the Tree of Life was not seen as the center, Satan could and did, through disobedience, elevate the tree of knowledge to fill that vacuum. Since he was the manipulator of her feelings and decisions, this put Satan at the center of her sight. From that error we inherit the mental rut of placing too much importance on the devil. *Satan is not at the center of life.* He is not God's opposite number. His power was never anywhere near equal to God's.

Life is *not* a battle between the forces of light and darkness. That is the Manichean heresy. In Jerusalem there is a museum which houses the Dead Sea Scrolls. Outside its walls is a huge, upright slab of white rock, opposed by several slabs of black. These are the sculptor's portrayal of the beliefs of the Essenes of that day. They believed that life is a contest between the forces of light (which they represented) and the forces of darkness. But that is heresy both to Jews and Christians. *Life is a pilgrimage in which Father God is raising children with whom to have fellowship in eternity.*

There happens also to be a struggle with the devil and his cohorts, but that is a *detail* of history, *not* the grand theme. The grand theme is the perfection of God's sons and daughters.

The devil did not necessitate the cross. Sin did. And that was not a slip-up that caused God to insert the cross as "Plan B" because Satan tempted Eve. Father God knew from the ground plan of creation that the price for His creatures to have free will in order to become sons and daughters would have to be the cross of Christ. Jesus *accomplished* the cross (Luke 9:31, John 4:34 and 5:36). *He did not succumb to it* because Satan "won a round" in the Garden of Eden. God's plan of transformation means that Satan wins *nothing*. He is not the moving force of history, nor is sin. God, and only God, is.

But Eve's error has set an engram of delusion into all our minds. How easy it is to celebrate the strength of the flesh rather than God's trans-forming power! When the Holy Spirit fell on main-line churches in the sixties and seventies, and we soon discovered that demons are real and that they do inhabit people, how quickly we saw demons in every person and behind every bush, whether they were there or not! All too often we still hear

ourselves saying, "The devil made me do it." Or
worship leaders routinely command the devil away
so that people can worship, when a little
discernment would have revealed that he was
nowhere around!

Or, worst of all from my point of view, too
many times ministries have wrongly concluded
that devils were present and have shouted at
supposed demons in people, wounding and frighten-
ing those poor hurting people, whereas it was not
demons but only flesh that should have been taken
gently by repentance to the cross in prayer. (Paula
and I have been involved in many valid exorcisms,
perhaps more than most servants of Christ alive
today. We are not speaking against recognizing the
reality of demonization and the occasional need for
real deliverances, but against foolish over-
emphasis.) *Mistaken over-emphasis happens for
many reasons, but first because Eve's error created
that track in our minds.*

The remedy is not to shout at the devil to leave
us alone, but to overcome him by the blood and by
the word of our testimony (Rev. 12:11). That means
simply to haul our "out-of-balancedness" to the
cross and to believe that the battle has been won
for us by our Lord once for all (1 John 2:13,14). We
need only to fasten our eyes on the Lord Jesus
Christ and celebrate His victory. *When we simply
turn to praise the Lord, He inhabits the praises of
His people — and the devil will have to flee, without
garnering any attention to himself.*

When we make evil more prevalent and powerful than it is, behind that is Eve's statement ". . . or touch it." Fear lies beneath that. Fear clouds the clarity of the mind and helps to prevent accurate recall of commands. Placing Satan at the center enhances the world of fear. Fear breeds lack of trust in those who protect us, most especially in our Father God. As we will see in a moment, Satan used that untrust to further beguile Eve. *But for now, let us see that the root of fear and untrust in us began at this point in history.* Trust, openness, courage, freedom to venture, even naivete are the natural instincts of our spirit by creation. *From Eve's error came deep ruts of untrust in all of us, stimulating closure, creating hearts of stone, fearfulness, patterns of flight, and unnatural deviousness and cleverness.*

We are, therefore, at root intrinsically ambivalent — alternately trusting and doubting, becoming vulnerable and closing off, possessing lion-hearts and fleeing when no enemy pursues (Prov. 28:1). We step out boldly where angels fear to tread, and in the next moment, like Elijah, flee from a mere woman (1 Kings 19)! One moment we walk blindly by faith as we should and the next moment we demand to know what is what, before we will take one more step (Hab. 2:4). Thus we are constantly at war:

> For I know that nothing good dwells within me, that is, in my flesh; for the wishing is present in me, but the doing of the good is not. For the good that I wish, I do not do; but I *practice* the very evil that I do not wish. *But if I am doing the*

> *very thing I do not wish, I am no longer the one*
> *doing it, but sin which dwells in me.* I find then
> the principle that evil is present *in* me, the one who
> wishes to do good. For I joyfully concur with the
> law of God in the inner man, but *I see a different*
> *law in the members of my body,* waging war
> against the law of my mind, *and making me a*
> *prisoner of the law of sin which is in my members.*
> (Rom. 7:18-23, italics mine)

St. Paul was talking, in his terms, of what we
have called engrams, deep ruts which cause
ambivalence at the core, leading us to "practice"
the very evils we deplore. But God has said,
through His apostle, in James 1:5-8:

> But if any of you lacks wisdom, let him ask
> of God, who gives to all men generously and
> without reproach, and it will be given to him. But
> let him ask in faith without any doubting, for the
> one who doubts is like the surf of the sea driven
> and tossed by the wind. For let not that man
> expect that he will receive anything from the Lord,
> *being a double-minded man, unstable in all his*
> *ways.* (Italics mine.)

Steadiness and Faithfulness

We need to be steadfast. Steadiness and
faithfulness are absolute prerequisites for anyone
who would mature in Christ. Therefore *this mental*
rut of fear and root of untrust lie at the very core
of destructiveness to our faith! Right there is the
foundation of back-sliding. *Ambivalence, what the*
Bible calls double-mindedness, is one of the
strongest, most firmly founded conditions of our
sinful nature.

We must win the war for the renewal of our minds on this battleground — or forget about vital and victorious faith. The answer could not be more simple. "Lord, let your perfect love cast out my fear (1 John 4:18), for you did not give me a spirit of timidity again to fear but "of power and love and discipline" (2 Tim. 1:7)! Lord, bring all that mentality of confusion and ambivalence to death on your cross, for you are not the author of my ambivalence and confusion." (See 1 Cor. 14:33).

That prayer may have to be reinforced many times, not because God didn't hear but because we don't want to let the prayer have full effect in us. "Who through fear of death were subject to slavery all their lives" (Heb. 2:15). Our minds fear to let go of control, and so prefer bondage rather than freedom! But "Thou wilt keep him in perfect peace whose *mind is stayed* on Thee" (Isa. 26:3, KJV, italics mine). Note: when prayer has settled the issue, our mind *is stayed* (passive tense), kept in line by the Lord himself, and the result is peace and rest.

The next error of Eve was induced by Satan, whether or not Adam properly instructed her. Having perceived fear behind Eve's mistakes, Satan moved to use that fear to his advantage. What he said was so obviously wrong, had Eve retained her rightful mind, she would have responded immediately, "That's not so. That's wrong. You're telling me a lie." He said, "You surely shall not die! For God knows that in the day you eat from it your eyes will be opened, and you will be like God, knowing good and evil" (Gen.

3:4,5). In saying, "You surely shall not die" Satan was directly telling Eve that God was lying to Adam when He said the penalty would be death.

Had Eve been feeding from the fruit of the Tree of Life, she would have felt within her our Lord's righteousness, His truthfulness and goodness. She would instantly have sensed something wrong, even if she did not yet recognize it mentally. Saying, "God knows. . . " implied that of course it would be good to have that fruit to eat, so "God just doesn't want the best for you like *I* do." Had she been filled with the fruit of the Tree of Life, she would have known in every fiber of her being that God wants the very best for us at all times! She would have rejected Satan's lies easily for what they were, "I *know* Him. He visits with us every night. *I feed on His nature every day.* He's not like what you are implying. You're a liar. I don't think I like you." But she had not been feeding where she should, and so she was vulnerable to Satan's lies and temptation.

In her defense, it should be said that this conversation was not at all fair, even had she been feeding rightly on Jesus. She was standing in the presence of the father of all lies and liars (John 8:44). There was nothing clean and objective about their conversation. Any woman who has experienced a lecherous man looking her up and down with lust knows what it is to feel defiled from head to toe. Any person who has done only a few exorcisms knows what it is to feel the nausea Satan's presence engenders. Defilement a thousand times worse than those small touches was flooding over Eve all the while she talked with Satan! His evil presence more and more effectively robbed her of her will power and clarity of thought the longer their conversation continued.

From this we can see our own vulnerability to defilement and temptation. Deeply bitter roots and false mental ruts have been handed down to us in two ways: *first* from the *lack of feeding* discussed earlier, and the consequent weakness of spirit, and *second* from *inherited tracks* of defilement, both as *bitter roots* from drinking from Satan's nature, and as *twisted ruts* of thoughts about God and His nature.

From Eve's deception, it is a "given" in us not to trust fully that God is as good as the Bible reveals Him to be. At root level, from Eve's deposit in us, and our own poor choices, we don't tap into His presence sufficiently nor frequently enough to cause every cell of our being to resonate with His goodness. If we did, we would for the most part be greatly immune to temptation and delusion. We don't yet know Him as we should. A large part of the reason for that lies here, in inherited, hidden habits of slothfulness in devotion, and thoughts of mistrust below the level of conscious thought. *We will not successfully recover freedom by mere determination to keep our prayer life going, or by fighting to keep our thoughts pure toward Him. Again, confession is in order:* "Father, I fail to be with you as I ought. Therefore, I don't trust you as I should. Bring my spiritually slothful and wandering nature to death on the cross. Give me a new heart of devotion, and a new mind of trust."

St. Paul warns:

> Do not be deceived: "Bad company corrupts good morals."Become *sober-minded* as you ought, and stop sinning; for some have no knowledge of God. I speak this to your shame. (1 Cor. 15:33,34, italics mine)

Bad Company

Because Eve kept bad company in the Garden, it is a root tendency in all of us to ally ourselves with people who do us little good! What parent has not been grieved and puzzled to see his otherwise normal and emotionally healthy child taking up with "orangutans" and other undesirable characters? We parents do the same, however. We know that there are people with whom we ought not to fellowship, but sometimes we seem to be fatally attracted to the very people who are apt to influence us wrongly.

In our mental ruts, we try to excuse our behavior, or think faint-heartedly that we ought to flee out of some of our relationships. But we fail to act as we should, much as Eve may have entertained second thoughts while she talked with Satan, but did not follow through.

Freedom is not achieved merely by determining to find better friends, though that may help. We need to crucify that in us which seeks the flattery of friendship with people weaker than ourselves in grace and wisdom, and to pray for the humility to seek out those friends whose fellowship will make us stretch to improve.

On his part, Satan was attempting to disengage Eve's roots from the righteous nurture of the Lord, and to attach her roots to himself. It needs to be understood that in direct ratio to time and increase of defilement, that much less was she able to think her own thoughts. Defilement works that way.

One moment we may rightly and perhaps pridefully congratulate ourselves that we are withstanding corruption and thinking our own thoughts clearly, and the next we may be totally swept away without knowing it. I learned that the hard way. At Drury College in Springfield, Missouri, my older brother Hal and I became involved in the only "panty raids" that ever happened in Drury's history! A panty raid was a massive invasion of women's dorms by male students for fun and mischief, which sometimes fell to vandalism.

Having been called out in the night to join in the fracas, and seeing what was going on, I decided to participate *partially*, hoping to help keep some order. At first I did. Having gained entrance to McCullough Cottage along with a score of others through a rear upstairs window, I merely watched as young men tossed beds upside down, swiped panties and bras from drying lines for trophies, teased the women and generally made mayhem. I remember seeing, with the calm detachment of "Star Trek's" Mr. Spock, that instead of simply opening the front door and walking out, my friends ran to a front window, not bothering to raise the venetian blinds, and stepped *through* them, out onto the front porch! I stopped, raised the blinds, visited with Mrs. Giles, the dorm mother, apologizing for the behavior of us all, said good night, and stepped onto the porch. So far so good, I was still in control of myself.

But then mob rule took over. I found myself marching with the crowd to the next dorm, shouting with them their obscenities — and wound up throwing gravel on the president's roof, laughing demoniacally. Later, when I returned to my senses, I repented and asked forgiveness of the Lord, as well as a few dozen others! Now, I praise God for that experience, for by it I can comprehend to some degree what happened to Eve — and how good people today can become carried away by such things as lynch mobs to do things that normally would be abhorrent to their conscience. At one moment we can be proceeding securely within our own thoughts, and the next, swept away in the onslaught of mob defilement, entirely overcome by satanic winds of feeling and thinking (Eph. 4:14).

The Battle for the Control of Men's Minds

The great warfare is the battle for the control of men's minds, especially in this modern day. Propagandists have learned to manipulate the media until entire masses of people have become brainwashed into doing whatever demagogues want them to do. Khomeini's religious fanatics sent mere children rushing mindlessly into mine fields, believing they would enter paradise through martyrdom in their leaders' false jihad (religious war).

Multitudes in the sixties tore apart Detroit and other cities in racial turmoils until those cities looked like battlefields in the aftermath of war. Today, we Christians often catch one another up in the latest delusion trumpeted in the mass media. For example, there was the hype and foolishness we went through when the teaching about prosperity went off balance for a while.

Worse, Satan works through principalities and world rulers of this present darkness (Eph. 6:12), to imprison and control all our thinking processes so as to prevent the Church from gaining the freedom and wisdom by which to crush his head as prophesied in Genesis 3:15.

Few Christians today realize how seldom the thoughts they think are truly their own in Christ, and how often they are unwittingly conformed to the world while thinking they are serving only the Lord. The plea here is for discipline, to be resolved to haul the mind daily to death in our fleshly feelings and thoughts, no longer carried to and fro by the cunning of men in deceitful wiles (Eph. 4:14). *Our propensity to be overtaken and made captive to do someone else's will began right there in Eve's succumbing to Satan's defilement.* It is dangerous to think oneself too educated or too wise to fall. We must daily take our own thoughts captive to obedience to Christ (2 Cor. 10:5).

Mass Defilement

I intentionally belabor this point because I know prophetically that the *warfare for the control of men's minds through mass defilement will increase and become the major battleground of our day.* That is certainly one strong message we can take as a rhema word from Rev. 12: 15: "And the serpent poured water like a river out of his mouth after the woman, so that he might cause her to be swept away with the flood."

Today, the ever-increasing capability to influence people through mass media has for the first time given the devil real opportunity to sweep the Church away in a veritable flood from his mouth — pornography, propaganda, false teachings in books, movies, VCRs, magazines, newspapers, etc. For just one example, today countless Christian couples think nothing of living together without benefit of marriage; something that would have been unthinkable a generation ago! Their minds have been swept away in the flood. *The day is coming when only those who pay the price of constant vigilance and daily death on the cross will stand free in our Lord Jesus Christ.*

Rooted in Love

One antidote to delusion deserves more attention. Had Eve been feeding on the Tree of Life, she would have been *rooted in love*, empowered to comprehend ". . . what is the breadth and length and height and depth, and to know the love of Christ which surpasses knowledge. . ." (Eph. 3:18,19, italics mine). The strength of her spirit would have arisen to throw off Satan's defilement.

How truly our Lord said, "Abide in Me, and I in you. As the branch cannot bear fruit of itself, unless it abides in the vine, so neither can you, unless you abide in Me" (John 15:4). Love not only casts off fear, it enables us to throw off defilement and delusion.

I have known many saints in the Lord who were neither educated nor very intelligent, but who were the wisest, most stable Christians I have met, more impervious to delusion and temptation than many brilliant scholars and theologians. Theirs were hearts of simple devotion and service to the Lord. They were, above all, loving people.

> *When the woman saw that the tree was good for food, and that it was a delight to the eyes, and that the tree was desirable to make one wise, she took from its fruit and ate; and she gave also to her husband with her, and he ate. (Gen. 3:6)*

With whose eyes was Eve now seeing? Satan's of course. Defilement had run its course in her. Today we would simply say she had become possessed. She was no longer thinking her own thoughts. Presumably the tree was in fact a delight to behold. If sin didn't look good, who would do it?!

Probably, God had intended later on, when they had become mature enough, to give them permission to eat its fruit. For example, when children are small, we do not tell them everything we know about sex. Not that there is anything wrong with sex, but our children are too young and immature to handle such knowledge rightly. In the same way, I'm sure our loving heavenly Father would have given us the fulness of knowledge of good and evil in His own time and way.

If this supposition is true, then Satan tempted Adam and Eve to take by force of sin what God would have given at the right time by grace. Certain it is that ever since then *we are all powerfully influenced by root tendencies and mental ruts to take again and again by force of sin what God would have given at the right time by grace.*

A fiance, who takes his beloved sexually before the marriage ceremony, has taken by force of sin that which God would have given him in holiness in the right time and way. A thief takes by force of sin the provision God could have given him in righteous ways. A liar tries to obtain by his lies what God might have found for him in godly ways.

Every sin we do has behind it untrust that the good God will provide what is best for us in His own time and way. That habit of falsely grabbing what we want, rather than waiting for the goodness of God to provide the best, is a mental rut of untrust we have all inherited from both Adam and Eve. Prayers for patience will help but won't get it done unless we also pray, "Lord, slay my false wantings and my untrust. Let me be born anew here too, equipped and empowered by your heart of trust in our heavenly Father."

> Then the eyes of both of them were opened, and they knew that they were naked; and they sewed fig leaves together and made themselves loin coverings. (Gen. 3:7)

If it is good for eyes to be opened, if we remember that God had commanded them not to eat of that tree, and now we see that their disobedience brought about something good, we have a problem! Matthew 7:17,18 says, "Even so, every good tree bears good fruit; but the bad tree bears bad fruit." God never said that the tree of the knowledge of good and evil was bad, only that Adam and Eve should not eat from its fruit. But the quandary still remains; *did a sinful act produce something good? From this confusion has come the mistaken notion that if we sin, something good will come of it!* Thinking to experience peace or to heighten their sensitivities, people get hooked on drugs! Men and women excuse their extra-marital affairs, saying, "I'm coming alive like never before!" (Actually, they're dying in their *souls,* while being *emotionally* excited and turned on.) "This is wonderful! Surely something this good can't be bad." *That sinful and foolish mental rut has seduced untold thousands into misery.*

Let it be known once for all, "Do not be deceived, God is not mocked; for whatever a man sows, this will he also reap. For the one who sows to his own flesh shall from the flesh reap corruption, but the one who sows to the Spirit shall from the Spirit reap eternal life" (Gal. 6:7,8). *Nothing good ever comes from sin!* Our Lord's grace may transform the results to better than what was before, but that is at the cost of His suffering, not the product of our sin.

Let's clear up the confusion. Adam and Eve now saw good and evil in the warped way Satan sees, not in the pure and wise way God perceives good and evil! *Nothing good came from their sin.* All their knowing, and all mankind's to follow, was unremittingly tainted from then on until redemption centuries later, with Satan's sick delusions of right and wrong! *All our confused mental tracks about wrongdoing stem from this one disobedience.* Let us never again think that any good thing comes from sinning! In this sense *their eyes were closed, not opened — closed to God's pure way of seeing and opened to Satan's insane versions of reality.* And so are ours, until the Father gives us the mind of Christ.

"...And she gave also to her husband with her, and he ate. *Then* the eyes of *both* of them *were opened.*" What a dramatic fact that until Adam also ate, nothing happened! Adam was in headship, both by being created first and by being her husband. Therefore, until his disobedience agreed with her sin, nothing resulted. Eve was deceived; Adam was not. God's gift of Eve had become so precious to him, he chose her before God! *From this sin derives our rut of choosing the woman in place of God.*

Any time a man listens inappropriately to his wife rather than to God, he has committed Adam's sin all over again. Whoever sins sexually with any woman has surrendered again to that track of placing a woman before God in importance; a rut built by Adam in this first sin of mankind. That rut has been the basic first cause for every man's sexual sins. All of us have it in us to fall to seduction. No one is safe. We cannot secure ourselves from making women too important, or from sexual sin, by castrating ourselves or by fleeing to a monastery or by gritting our teeth to hang on to moral virtue, though the latter may help. Rather we need to pray, *"Dear God, bring this 'rutting' nature of mine to death. Set me free in you to have emotions and think and act in relation to women as only you would have me do."*

"...And they knew they were naked." However long *Adam and Eve had lived in the Garden before the Fall, they knew all that time that they were naked. As Genesis 2:25 carefully states it, "... the man and his wife were both naked and were not ashamed."* But now they knew their nakedness as Satan knows it — in lust and filthiness! Now they were ashamed. We see the change in them immediately — they covered themselves with fig leaves.

From this mental rut has originated all our tendency to pornography, "adult" bookstores (in actuality quite juvenile), R-rated and X-rated movies, and so on. Porno can grab hold of its victims primarily because that rut is there from Adam's immediate wrong beholding of Eve when Satan's sinful way entered their hearts. "For all that is in the world, the lust of the flesh and *the lust of the eyes* and the boastful pride of life, is not from the Father, but is *from the world"* (1 John 2:16, italics mine). St. John could as easily have said, "... is from that deposit into our natures from Adam and Eve's sin."

We have counseled so many who have pitifully struggled by determination for years, failing again and again to find freedom from whatever form lust took in their lives. They discovered joyous freedom when they stopped struggling in the flesh and simply prayed, "Lord, you have already won this battle for me. I claim that victory, and I rest in your ability to keep me safe from harm." To be sure, they had to exercise some will power, but now their will was being directed to stand *in Jesus* rather than merely to struggle on futilely in the flesh. They had to learn not to empower the flesh by the strength of the law (Rom. 7:8), and how to believe and trust in Jesus, but they got free.

7

Roots and Ruts Devolved From Adam and Eve's Sinful Replies to God in the Garden of Eden

> And they heard the sound of the Lord God walking in the garden in the cool of the day, and the man and his wife hid themselves from the presence of the Lord God among the trees of the garden. Then the Lord God called to the man, and said to him, *"Where are you?"* (Gen. 3:8,9, italics mine)

Could anyone suppose that the omniscient Lord of all the universe did not in fact know where Adam was? When a psychiatrist enters the room of a mentally ill patient, he may say, "Where are you today?" And/or "Who are you today?" If the person can respond, "I'm Sam Smith and I am in _____ Mental Institution" and that is in fact who and where he is, his declaration has strengthened his hold on reality — and has informed the psychiatrist about his state of health. Of course our loving heavenly Father knew where Adam and Eve were; He was attempting to give them a chance to come forward and confess what they had done. Had they done so, all of history would have been different! However, God in His foreknowledge knew that they would not. Nevertheless, He gave them every opportunity.

Imagine time, and silence, as God waited, loving Adam, willing him to come forward, knowing all along where he was and what he had done.

But Adam was afraid.

I doubt that this was the first time God had come walking in the cool of the day. The context seems to indicate a habit of relaxing in the Garden, visiting with Adam and Eve. Each time before, most likely Adam and Eve had come running like delighted children do when their daddy comes home from work. How Adam and Eve's hearts must have leaped with joy at the sound of His coming! Nothing heretofore had clouded their spirits' perception of His love and graciousness. They knew Him. As an old Latvian hymn says, they could ". . . walk and talk with Him and jest, as good friends should and do."

But now their roots had become dislodged by sin from God's gentle nurture; and Satan's doubt and guiltiness had perverted their comprehension of Him. His presence now brought fear, rather than the comfort of homecoming.

Early on in my walk with Christ, I came to understand a bit of what Adam and Eve felt. God heard my prayer, soon after my conversion, and caught me up into the very glory of His presence before His throne in heaven. But I was too young in faith to trust fully in the blood of Jesus to cover all my sin. His awesome, utterly holy golden glory shot all through me, revealing in its passage my sinfulness and shame. *I was TERRIFIED!* Whatever God might have revealed or said to me, I never knew. I fought to escape from that terrible holy presence until I found myself sitting again at my desk in my office.

But I had 2,000 years of Christianity behind me, plus a most recent experience of salvation. To catch a glimmer of Adam and Eve's situation, remove from your mind those centuries of God's expressed forgiveness through the blood of the cross, mix in a most recent experience of Satan's defiling presence, add the terror of their guilt before anything was known about forgiveness — perhaps then we can begin to understand why they fled from the very personification of forgiveness and healing!

(And the Scriptures don't tell us whether God had taught them what to do if they sinned in some way, or even if they happened to sin unintentionally.)

Fear of God's Presence

Out of their flight from God comes one of the most powerful ruts in all our thinking! We say we want God to meet us in our corporate worship and private devotions, but *the truth is that we don't want Him to come any closer than we can control and feel comfortable about.* We're *afraid* of His awesome presence.

Were God to reveal to us how many times He has wanted to approach us and how often we have fled away from prayer before He could, we would probably be shocked beyond belief!

Frequently, while traveling to church after church, Paula and I have participated in worship services in which we could sense the imminent approach of God upon His people — and have witnessed how often congregations and leaders have changed the subject and fled away before He could come in His fulness! Has anyone failed to notice in the Scriptures that almost every time an angel appeared to a servant of God, the first words out of his mouth were "Fear not!"? No wonder! We're terrified of the holy!

We're not merely afraid of His presence — we're afraid to come forward and confess our sins. Probably any counselor can recall instances of counselees calling to cancel appointments because, as they later admitted, they knew in their hearts that things were surfacing which needed that day to be confessed. Often, when a person has been ripening to face some "awful" thing, he or she has fled out of the counseling office — or did not come at all that day. We come by those "flight patterns" honestly — we got them from Adam and Eve before we were born!

Patterns of Flight and Alibis

For every flight pattern, we possess built-in excuses. Did you ever notice how easy it is to find a reason not to confess something? "Perfect" alibis pop out of our mouths before we even have a chance to think. We don't have to strive to make alibis, they just pop out! *Mental ruts of flight and alibi-making supply our tongues with words from data-banks as old as Adam standing before God,* saying:

"I heard the sound of Thee in the garden, and I was afraid *because I was naked;* so I hid myself." (Gen. 3:10, italics mine)

Is that why Adam was afraid? Of course not. He was afraid because he had sinned, and Satan had robbed him of ability to trust in God's loving nature. So he put the wrong reason on his foolish actions. That deception built into all mankind *the deep mental track of putting lying reasons behind foolish deeds.* From this, let me lay out a maxim for all counselors to follow: *Never allow a noble reason for foolishness or sin.* Good produces good. Evil produces evil. More to the point, good cannot produce evil, and *evil cannot produce good.*

For example, a wife insists that her husband talk with us because "He has been punishing the children too heavily. Sometimes his discipline is really abuse!"

He says, "Well, I got into a lot of trouble as a kid, and I know what can happen. I guess I just love my kids too much. I'm determined to keep them out of trouble."

True determination, born of love, would have created compassion and teaching rather than abuse. Our probing soon reveals that his father greatly abused him when he was a child. Unforgiveness now caused him to do the same thing to his own children (Rom. 2:1). *Evil created the abuse; lovingkindness cannot act like that.*

A wife brought her husband (Fred, in the first chapter) to us because at a party the night before, when a man made some lewd advances towards her, he reacted with horrible violence rather than with protective wisdom. "I guess I just love her too much, so I lost my head when that guy treated her like that." Love, being good, can never produce evil. The Holy Spirit soon uncovered that his mother had been unfaithful. He had never yet dealt with his angers at the man who had seduced his mother, or with his disappointment and judgments toward her, now projected upon his wife.

The most common example by far is: "I just couldn't help myself when I went to bed (with someone in fornication or adultery); I'm just head over heels in love." Wrong! Nothing but lust overcame moral conscience! Truly Christian love would have carried with it respect for the other in the sight of God.

Evil Motives — Evil Deeds

The understanding that evil motives always lie behind evil deeds can serve as a most effective lie detector for every counselor. "For the word of God is living and active and sharper than any two-edged sword, and piercing as far as the division of soul and spirit, of both joints and marrow, and *able to judge the thoughts and intentions of the heart*" (Heb. 4:12, italics mine). "The testimony of the Lord is sure, *making wise the simple*" (Ps. 19:7b, italics mine). The simple truth that good things can never lie behind bad deeds has helped me unravel thousands of Gordian knots in counseling!

We learned the track of lying to ourselves before we learned anything, because we never *had* to "learn" it; it came with the package of being human, an engram from Adam's first lie to God, "because I was naked." There is no other way to get rid of it than by the cross. God doesn't intend to fix it; He intends to slay it — and has done so already, on the cross of Christ. Our response? "Slay it in me, Lord. Set me free from deceiving myself and others. Give me a heart and mind of truth and honesty."

God saw the deception in Adam's reply, but said nothing about it. I doubt that He needed to. I can remember being a ten-year-old, standing before my dad, having trotted out my latest lame-brained excuses. The silence had been deafening with the thunder of revelation! Kindness and sternness flickered alternately across his face, teased by barely repressed chuckles. I couldn't help but see the lies behind my protestations. And likewise, Adam knew his lie hadn't worked!

So God tried again, this time a little more directly: "Who told you that you were naked" (Gen. 3:11a)? Picture God waiting patiently again — let's not press on to His next question for a while. Imagine our loving heavenly Father standing there pouring love throughout Adam's heart and mind and spirit, wooing him, hoping, like so many earthly fathers later on, to endow his child with enough courage to confess what he had done. God was trying to re-attach Adam's roots to himself, his heavenly Father.

We know from Adam's silence, and his wrong answer to the next question, that God didn't win. So we might ask, "Why?" God had all the power of the universe. Why did Satan succeed in keeping Adam's mind enthralled? Because God is a gentleman and Satan is not! God will never force His good will on any person, nor use His power to control, over-influence or manipulate, even though He knows that not to use His power may allow a dearly beloved child to fall to ever greater suffering in sin. That is the price even an omniscient God must pay if He would have sons and daughters rather than robots.

But Satan *will* use anything he can lay hold of to get his own selfish way — possession, blinding (2 Cor. 4:4), hypnotism (Deut. 18:11), manipulation, trickery and cunning in interpreting God's Word (2 Cor. 4:2), temptation, thought-control, whatever. There was nothing fair about the contest for the free will of Adam, just as there is nothing fair in the warfare for men's souls today — but what a comfort that ". . . this is the will of Him who sent Me, that of all He has given Me *I lose nothing,* but raise it up on the last day" (John 6:39, italics mine).

From Adam's silence to God's question, we inherit our own reluctance and rebellious resistance to responding as we should in hundreds of situations! How about all those times we have seen brothers or sisters actually swaying back and forth physically as they fought *not* to respond to God at an altar call? Or the times when we knew God's Holy Spirit was prompting us to give a word, or make a confession, and we stood there silently sweating while our heart pumped harder and harder? Or all those occasions when we knew in our spirit, and even at the edges of our mind, that it was really God who was prompting us to make an apology to our mate or some other loved one — but we stood stubbornly, fearfully silent? *We suffer that kind of mental imprisonment from deep ruts installed by Adam's silence before the patience of God!*

Personal Responsibility

However, we can't get away with blaming it all on poor old Adam, as though we were nothing but victims. We inherit mental ruts of seduction without asking for them, but *they do not become controlling forces until we surrender to them and act upon them. We are always responsible for our sin. We choose* to act upon the evil promptings of our hearts. To find freedom, we need to see that the propensity to stubborn silence and withdrawal started there in Eden. *It ends when we see its rootage in selfishness and fear and determine to kill its power over us by the cross of Christ.*

As children, we added another dimension to this habit, or at least I did. I learned how to get my mother's goat by "turning off" and remaining silent while she upbraided me and demanded answers. I learned that by not showing any kind of emotion at all, I could push her clean out of control — and that kind of wicked power felt good! Later, as a Christian trying to become more like my Lord, I found that I had to become willing to see my malicious delight for what it was and to come to hate it enough to quit using that childish technique on Paula and others close to me. Do you suppose I am the only sinner who does that? I doubt it.

When Adam didn't answer, God tried again, this time much more directly: "Have you eaten from the tree of which I commanded you not to eat" (Gen. 3:11b)? Can anyone believe our omniscient Lord didn't already know the answer to His question? Why then did He ask? He wanted to give Adam and Eve every chance to come clean before Him.

Can anyone who knows the Lord believe He shouted His questions with fury and rancor, as a human father sometimes might? No. With pain in His heart for Adam and Eve, how gently He must have questioned them. But Adam and Eve were now under the influence of Satan. Have we not all seen how often frightened and guilty children perceive their parents' tender and gentle questioning as vehemence and threats? Adam and Eve had become deaf to the real nature of God's voice. They now dreaded what ought to have comforted them.

Just so, today, innumerable parishioners hear malicious attacks in the loving rebukes of pastors whose hearts are breaking in love for them! *That deep rut of the mind wreaks havoc in church after church, Sunday after Sunday.* Not that some pastors don't do some faulty accusatory preaching, but if we were free from this rut inherited from the first ones who listened to God, we would be capable of hearing God's truth no matter how faulty His vessels, and so we would be grateful to God for caring enough to discipline us (Heb. 12:5-11).

That same rut works rebellion and hatred between parents and children, bosses and employees, officers and enlisted personnel, and so on, *ad nauseam.* God is waiting still for a people willing to pay the price of self-death in order to grow up into a mighty army, united in Him, rather than peevish children who continue to quibble in self-justifying, self-seeking ways.

Passing the Buck

Finally, Adam knew he had to respond — and so he came up with the first instance of buck-passing in the history of the world! "The *woman* whom *Thou* gavest to be with me, she gave me from the tree, and I ate" (Gen. 3:12, italics mine). Adam actually passed the buck twice — first onto Eve, and second, onto God himself!

God, being the essence of kindness He is, passed over Adam's foolish response and turned to the woman: "What is this you have done" (Gen. 3:13a)? — as though He didn't know already. But Eve only came up with history's second instance of buck-passing! "The serpent deceived me, and I ate" (Gen. 3:13b).

Thus, we inherit a *double dose* of buck-passing! We get it from both our progenitors. Rare is the man or woman who can stand and take even the mildest accusations without attempting to alibi, excuse, rationalize, or pass the buck somewhere. Silly excuses and blaming of others just seem to flow so easily out of our mouths! That habit never had to be taught to us; it came with our skin and bones, grafted into our nature. Again, we'll not get free by becoming determined "never to do that again." Galatians 2:20 and 5:24 are the only answer. We must attempt to crucify our buck-passing nature so persistently that He finally takes pity and does it for us.

Adam's "...whom *Thou* gavest to be with me," was of course an attempt to blame God for his own sin. What a pervasive and powerful rut that has built into all of us! When tragedies happen, even our secular law courts proclaim, "An act of God!" Deaths and tragedies happen, and people cry out, "Why did God do this to me?" Proverbs 19:3 says, "When a man's folly brings his way to ruin, his heart rages against the Lord" (RSV).

In the depths of our spirit, as we said earlier, we want to tell God that life and His purposes aren't fair. For this reason St. Paul wrote, "Therefore, we are ambassadors for Christ, as though God were entreating through us; we beg you on behalf of Christ, *be reconciled to God*" (2 Cor. 5:20, italics mine). Note that in this instance, the Word does not speak of God being reconciled to us, but the other way around — as though we need to forgive God. True! Of course God has never done anything deserving to be forgiven, but that doesn't keep us from being perfectly angry at a perfect God.

When my brother Hal was in kindergarten, all members of his class were to bring hard-boiled eggs to school for an Easter celebration. Hal came home that day furious at mom because she had never taught him how to break eggs against his forehead, and he was afraid that the yellow and white would run all down his face, and he didn't know how to keep that from happening, so he didn't get to eat any, and it was all her fault! Our angers at God are just that silly, but also terribly real to us.

We need to express forgiveness to God, knowing that what actually happens is that we *receive* forgiveness for our own foolish judgments against Him. We should pray, "Lord, bring this habit of blaming you in my heart to death on your cross (whether I can admit it in my mind or not), and resurrect trust and honor for you until that becomes second nature to me."

Passing over what God said to the serpent, let's move on to examine what He said to Eve:

I will greatly multiply your pain in childbirth, In pain you shall bring forth children; yet *your desire shall be for your husband, And he shall rule over you.* (Gen. 3:16, italics mine)

Some think that God was exacting vengeance, or punishing Eve. I doubt that. When I had done some sinful thing as a child, and my father had found out about it, he would sit me down and we would have a little talk. If he saw that I would have to reap some terrible consequences for what I had done, that was the end of his disciplining me. He would just tell me, "Son, this is what you are going to have to reap." He would explain to me in compassion what was going to happen, wanting me to understand, wishing me to derive the benefit of what I was about to learn through the "school of hard knocks." Far kinder than my earthly father, God was laying out before Adam and Eve what would be the consequences of their actions, so that they would understand, and grow in wisdom from their experiences.

There is some pain in all childbirth. God was explaining to Eve that her sin had set such tension into her body that her pain would increase. So it is that Eve's sin has set such a mold in our deep minds that women suffer great pains in childbirth. Today, Lamaze and Bradley methods are teaching women how to relax, lessening the pain of childbirth — but the best relaxer is still a clear conscience, made so by the art of confessing life's daily irritations and sins as they happen, moment by moment, abiding in the love of Jesus.

"Yet your desire shall be for your husband..." Desire already existed for her husband, both because she had been created from his rib and naturally felt incomplete without him, and because she had known no life without Adam. In His wisdom, God gave Adam only enough time without Eve to become lonely enough to want her. But Eve knew no life apart from her husband! Now, God was revealing to her that her sin would cause her desire for her husband to become inordinate. *Because she had caused her husband to choose her before God, she and her descendants would reap a perpetual rut of striving to please men rather than God!*

So many times Paula and I have heard women who thought they loved the Lord with all their hearts, brokenly confessing to adultery. Or recognizing that they had so often discarded their own better judgment, and had done some wrong thing their husbands had talked them into.

Worse yet, we have often grieved to hear of preachers and elders telling *women they must do whatever their husbands dictate,* believing that is what a truly submissive Christian wife must do — and wives, beguiled by this deep rut of desire to please the man, submitting and agreeing to that nonsense! God expects *every* person to use his own conscience and his own good common sense. We see this in principle in His advice concerning listening to prophets:

> If a prophet or a dreamer of dreams arises among you and gives you a sign or a wonder, and the sign or wonder comes true, concerning which he spoke to you, saying, "Let us go after other gods (whom you have not known) and let us serve them," *you shall not listen to the words of that prophet or that dreamer of dreams [or husband]; for the Lord your God is testing you* to find out if you love the Lord your God with all your heart and with all your soul. *You shall follow the Lord your God and fear Him; and you shall* keep His commandments, listen to His voice, serve Him, and cling to Him. (Deut. 13:1-4, italics mine)

If we can see that we ought not to listen to any prophet, or to any pastor or teacher who teaches wrongly, nor to do what he says if it is scripturally wrong, can we not see that the same principle applies to the obedience of wives to their husbands? When a command of the Lord is clear, a wife must follow God first, rather than her husband. This means that when a husband tells his wife, for example, that she is forbidden to attend church, he is out of line. *Husbands cannot be allowed to exercise authority which overrides the commandments of God.* He cannot be allowed to force her to lie, or cheat, or steal, or give herself sexually in wrong ways. Let every woman surrender to the Lord her tendency to please and obey her husband rather than God, and let her ask to be set free from that idolatry.

"And he shall rule over you." Adam was already established in headship over Eve, both by being the first created and by being her husband. In true godly rule, leaders lay down their lives in order to set free and enable all within their domain to become the most they can be in the Lord. A husband must never dominate and control, or use his position for personal advantage, or disrespect and treat his wife as an object or chattel to be used as he sees fit.

Historically, what God was prophesying to Eve has come to pass wherever the grace of Christ has not yet personally overcome the results of this first sin. Men have dominated and controlled women the world over! In most Moslem countries a woman can not vote, and her words will not even be heard in court, much less ever be allowed to override any man's testimony.

She is her husband's possession. If he beats her, the courts will say nothing; she is only a woman, and he has a right to do anything to her he wants to. Her children do not belong to her, or even to them, but only to him.

Wherever heresy enters a Christian group, one of the first and most telling signs is that women immediately lose their rights as free and equal partners and become second-class citizens from whom only slavish obedience is to be expected — in meek and submissive silence! Witness what happened when shepherding and discipling went off-balance a few years ago. We are still mopping up after that destruction of Christian family roles.

Eight months before I was born, before my mother knew she was pregnant with me, God spoke to her and told her that she was to have a son who would be His servant in many places and ways. Eliciting only a grunt from my father when she woke him to tell him what had happened, she thereby gained some wisdom, and told no one, least of all me. At eighteen, I declared for the ministry and preached my first sermon. That afternoon she sat me down and told me how I had been called from before my birth.

When it began to appear that Paula and I were becoming serious about one another, I told her there was a call on my life, and I would follow that call no matter what else. If that responsibility called me away from her, she needed to understand that at the outset. I thought I alone had a call, and Paula shared it only by being married to me.

The Lord then began to work on my male arrogance. After a while, He showed me that Paula is my partner in the Gospel. But I still thought it was my mission, and she had come along to be my helper. But *Paula is my helpmeet, not my helper.* Finally, the Lord showed me that *from the ground-plan of creation we had been created for the same mission.* It had always been *ours,* not mine with a helper. She is my full and equal partner.

Headship means that the buck stops with me, and that when we have not had sufficient time or cannot arrive at a decision together, I must make it, and face the consequences. From the struggle God went through to break me out of that rut inherited from Adam and Eve, so that I would agree to all that and embrace it, I know in some small part how deeply ingrained it is in all men to put women down, ever so subtly sometimes, but down nevertheless!

Our Lord Jesus Christ intends to restore Woman to more than she was in Eden. *He is the greatest "women's libber" of all time!* But He intends to do it by bringing this mental rut of dominance and control to death on His cross, not merely by marches and demonstrations. *He changes us from the inside out. Any other changes, in government, cultural patterns, theological and societal beliefs, etc. will have no lasting effect without death and rebirth. That is the meat and importance of these chapters, and the reason for this entire book!*

To Adam, God said:

> *Because you have listened to the voice of your wife, and have eaten from the tree about which I commanded you, saying, "You shall not eat from*

it"; Cursed is the ground because of you; In toil
you shall eat of it all the days of your life. Both
thorns and thistles it shall grow for you; and you
shall eat the plants of the field; By the sweat of
your face you shall eat bread, till you return to the
ground, because from it you were taken; For you
are dust, and to dust you shall return. (Gen. 3:17-19)

Adam had already been toiling. Before Eve
came to join him, he was at work taking care of the
Garden. Labor was meant to be nothing but
blessing. Heretofore, it had been. God had *enjoyed*
creating, and had pronounced each day's work
"good" (Gen. 1:4,10,12,18,21,25), and when all had
been created, *"very* good" (Gen. 3:31). But sin's
results would now fill labor with anxiety and
tension, creating "sweat." Physically, sweat is
good. Whoever cannot sweat in hot climates is in
trouble. God was saying that this kind of sweat
would not be good, originating from false struggles
in the flesh, from fear, anger and hatred. Later,
priests in the Temple were required to wear linen
to prevent sweating in the Lord's service (Ezek.
44:18). *Labor from Adam's time until redemption*
in our Lord has been corrupted by the curse of the
mental rut of strain which God prophesied here.

A Man's Two Worlds

It is greatly significant that Adam knew the
blessing of labor before Eve appeared, especially
that he knew labor as a secure blessing before his
involvement with her got him into sin. *Because of*
sinful ruts in men's thinking, from then until now
men tend to flee from their wives into the security
and manageable satisfaction of their work! A man

has two worlds: work and family — and all too often his family comes in a distant second. A woman, desiring her husband, even if her job also becomes a career, is still more likely to keep her priorities straight and put her family first.

Early on, the Lord took pains to make Paula and me aware of the seduction of the call of labor away from family. Though He had called us to be among those who work to restore the office of the prophet in the Church today, and to rediscover and define inner healing, and to labor to return families to biblical living, etc., He made it unmistakably clear that our first calling was and is to raise our six children unto the Lord!

Presidents soon will be almost forgotten. Best-selling novels will soon gather dust. Empires will crumble. However, if a man and his wife have but two children, whatever they build into them in the nature of precious stones, gold and silver (Christian character, wisdom and knowledge) will last forever in the hearts and minds of those children in heaven (1 Cor. 3:12). *Forming our children in the Lord may be our only truly eternal work.*

Whether it was due to the seductive call of labor, or some other causes, Adam and Eve did not do a good job of parenting — their first child committed the first murder! I grieve as I counsel leaders and their families, for far too frequently their children's lives have been sacrificed to the call of labor. "P.K.s" (preachers' kids) are known throughout Christendom for the frequency of rebellion and trouble in their lives.

Putting Our Priorities in Order

Though labor for Adam became filled with strain and sweat, *it was still his first love.* I plead with every brother and sister in Christ to put your priorities in order. Place your children next only to God in importance — God will not call you to serve Him in ways that destroy your children's lives. I plead with men, don't frustrate your wife's love for you by making her an occupational widow, jealous of your work. *Bring to death on the cross that practiced rut that came from Adam's loving his work first. Love your wife and family first after God, not your work.*

Sin separates. Immediately after they had sinned, guilt, fear and lies separated Adam and Eve from God. Then they were separated from each other by Eve's inordinate desire and the corruption of headship, and by Adam's preferring labor more than Eve. Finally they were separated from nature by thorns and thistles and unrewarding labor.

It became a vicious cycle which we inherit through roots and ruts today. Men spend too much time and energy at work. That frustrates their wives' desire to be with them. So wives scold or harangue or manipulate, trying to cause their husbands to pay them more attention. That makes husbands want to flee to the office or farm or factory, where they can feel more competent and composed, where they know how to make things happen and feel the satisfaction of seeing a job well done. That in turn disappoints their wives all the more, and their resultant bitterness, loneliness and tension cause them to act in ways which can only separate them further!

It is important for husbands and wives to see this cycle and come to hate it until both can haul it to the cross together. We need to repent of it as our own sin, and as a death-dealing cycle we have all inherited from our forefathers, generation to generation, back to Adam and Eve. It needs to be broken at the foot of the cross in repentance.

> *Then the Lord God said, "Behold, the man has become like one of us, knowing good and evil; and now, lest he stretch out his hand, and take from the tree of life, and eat, and live forever. . . (Gen. 3:22, italics mine)*

This text is perhaps the most greatly misunderstood passage in the Bible. Most of us have heard Sunday school teachers proclaiming that Adam and Eve had now become like God, knowing good and evil. I have heard professors in seminary courses in theology and biblical exegesis declare that Adam and Eve's sin was ". . . a fall upstairs, necessary if we were to become knowledgeable and wise!" Nothing could be more mistaken! Through this confusion we have built into ourselves at subconscious levels the foolish notion that if we sin, somehow we will become nobler and wiser, more like God.

Let us set the record straight. The scenario is as follows: God's angels have been watching God and Adam and Eve and the serpent who is Satan. God has in effect been holding court. He has not only been trying to save Adam and Eve from their error, He has been examining them before the court of heaven. All have seen that every time God has asked Adam and Eve a question, their answers have been fraught with deception, lies, alibis and buck-passing.

Satan long before had become corrupt and had fallen from grace, but he was still allowed access to the councils of heaven. In Job's time, he was still walking on the earth, and present in the council at which God said to him, "From where do you come?" And Satan answered, "From roaming about on the earth and walking around on it" (Job 1:7). Satan was not finally cast out of heaven's councils until the Lord sent out the seventy to preach the kingdom and they returned with rejoicing, and the Lord exclaimed, "I was watching Satan fall from heaven like lightning" (Luke 10:18).

Therefore, the examination of Adam and Eve being concluded, God said, "Behold, the man has become like one of us" (Gen. 3:22). Adam and Eve now knew good and evil, but not in the pure way God knows good and evil. They had come to know good and evil only as Satan knows good and evil. Their lies and sins had caused them to become spiritually, emotionally and mentally like Satan, not like God.

Please, let us hear it once for all, **we can never become more like God by sinning!!!** Sin makes us childish, not childlike. Evil produces only evil. Sin never makes people more noble and wise; it only makes them more foolish and rebellious.

Sinning Cannot Produce Good

From the misinterpretation of that text has descended a most persistent lie, a rut of deception that has done untold harm in the lives of countless people — that sinning somehow produces good. That lie weakens our resolve to stand in righteousness — after all, if I am going to become more like God by giving in to this or that temptation, why not?!

This erodes belief that God's laws mean what they say — after all, if Adam and Eve were rewarded by becoming like God through sinning, why should I expect to reap anything bad by doing something forbidden? That lie destroys trust in the nature of God — "He said that they would surely die, but they only became more like himself! I guess He didn't mean what He said."

When we have taught this lesson in seminars, I have been amazed to see how few realize the seriousness and tremendous impact of this error in the minds and lives of men and women everywhere. Let me encourage you to think long and hard, to meditate deeply about these things. You may see that this mental rut acts like a slimy snake slithering through the corridors of your mind, offering the same temptations to you as to Eve, until you see whatever sin looms before you as "...desirable to make one wise," "...a delight to the eyes," "...good for food."

We sin because whatever forbidden thing we want seems to be worth the price of sin to get it. The lure of it, and the lie that there won't be any bad consequences, and the foolishness of unconsciously thinking that we will be better people because of it — all come from this mental rut of thinking that God said Adam and Eve had become more like Him by sinning!

If we need more proof, had Adam and Eve truly become more like one of the Trinity, why put them out of the Garden, away from the Tree of Life? God *had* to put them out. Before they had sinned, their eating from the Tree of Life would have strengthened them in righteousness. But when sin corrupted their natures to become like Satan's, God could not let them feed again, lest what they had become be made eternal.

God could not let them return to the Garden until His Son's cross could purify them to live again among holy things. Here lies the crux of all our teaching: it is not enough merely to receive Jesus Christ as Lord and Savior. That *does* get us to heaven. But conversion only *begins* the process of death and rebirth required to prepare us for fulness of life in Jesus. *Positionally* it is all done (John 19:30). *Experientially* we must daily make His death for us more and more our own. *These chapters have been an effort to reveal to the Body of Christ what it is that needs to be called to death at the deepest levels in all of us.*

If readers do not make a conscious discipline of praying these things to death on the cross, this entire three chapters on roots and ruts shall have only entertained — or bored. I suggest, therefore, now that you have read them through once, *go back through these chapters at your leisure.* Take time to think through how each root and mental rut has been effective in your own life, and wrestle each one to the cross in prayer. It's wisest to do that in the company of other pilgrims, who can reveal to you how well you are doing.

Here, at the foot of the cross, moment by moment, day by day, is where we are either *transformed* according to God's Word — or *conformed* to the world! *Let's fight the battle where it counts — in the deep recesses of the mind!*

8

Restoring the Functions
of Mind and Heart
By R. Loren Sandford

> For who among men knows the thoughts of
> a man except the spirit of the man, which is in
> him? Even so the thoughts of God no one knows
> except the Spirit of God. Now we have received,
> not the spirit of the world, but the Spirit who is
> from God, that we might know the things freely
> given to us by God, which things we also speak,
> not in words taught by human wisdom, but in
> those taught by the Spirit, combining spiritual
> thoughts with spiritual words. But a natural man
> does not accept the things of the Spirit of God; for
> they are foolishness to him, and he cannot
> understand them, because they are spiritually
> appraised. But he who is spiritual appraises all
> things, yet he himself is appraised by no man. For
> WHO HAS KNOWN THE MIND OF THE
> LORD, THAT HE SHOULD INSTRUCT HIM?
> But we have the mind of Christ. (1 Cor. 2:11-16)

If we have the mind of Christ, what needs to
be renewed? What is dysfunctional in our minds?
And what does this renewal have to do with
proving the will of God? One major problem is that
the relationship between our minds and hearts has
been perverted, the roles confused. The proper
function of the mind in relation to the heart is to

make decisions, while the heart is to sense and feel things as the servant of the Spirit-renewed mind. Though we have the mind of Christ, too many of us don't yet walk in it.

The Function of the Heart

Let's first look at the function of the heart. Throughout the Scriptures, the heart is represented as merry, glad, stubborn, exultant, hateful, spiteful, loving and so on. In other words, the heart feels, intuits and understands things in a way unique among our other faculties. The heart also serves a pondering function and can achieve a level of understanding deeper than comprehension of mere facts. "Incline your heart to understanding" (Prov. 2:2). "The heart of the righteous ponders how to answer" (Prov. 15:28).

But because the heart is the seat of our fallen emotions, we are specifically instructed *not* to follow after it. Numbers 15:39 commands us not to follow after our own hearts, but to seek after the commandments of the Lord. Proverbs 28:26 says, "He who trusts in his own heart is a fool." The heart is not to be trusted. *Clearly the heart must not become the decision-maker in our lives.* Feelings change with daily body chemistry — what you ate for breakfast, how much sleep you got the night before, or whether your spouse picked on you today. Hardly the stuff of solid decision-making!

In fact, "The heart is more deceitful than all else" (Jer. 17:9). What an extreme statement! Although every aspect of the human condition has fallen from its original glory, the Scriptures tell us that the heart is more deceitful than any other part of us, more likely to mislead, more likely to misrepresent itself and to tell lies. Left to itself, the heart is the most selfish and, therefore, the most dishonest instrument we possess.

The Function of the Mind

What about the mind? The function of the mind is to know objectively and then to decide what to do with what is known. The mind, not the heart, functions to set direction, to make decisions and then to summon all other faculties to follow after. In order to accomplish this task on balance, the mind should be "set on the Spirit" (Rom.8:6), which is a decision, something the mind is designed for. In God's plan, the Holy Spirit rules the mind, and the mind directs the heart.

Listen to how the Scriptures put it, "My mind instructs me in the night" (Ps. 16:7). It teaches the rest of me, absorbing information, and identifying the objective truth of God's Word. "The mind of the intelligent seeks knowledge" (Prov. 15:14). By deciding to seek after knowing, the mind sets direction. "The mind of man plans his way, but the Lord directs his steps" (Prov. 16:9). The function of the mind is to plan, to set a righteous direction and then to marshall all the other parts of the person to pursue the chosen direction. In Romans 7 Paul laments the war going on within him. The law of sin wages war against the law of his mind. Again it is the mind attempting to function properly in setting a righteous direction.

The will of God is proved by a renewed mind because such a mind seeks out the truth and fulfills its function as the decision-maker, demanding that the other faculties, and especially the heart, live and function within the boundaries set by the decision. So the heart feels and intuits, while the mind knows and decides.

We get into trouble when the heart is allowed to become the decision-maker and judge of truth and the mind becomes carnal, the servant of the heart to justify and fortify what the heart has purposed. The mind should set borders and limits for the heart so that the heart becomes the compassionate servant of the renewed mind. When the mind fails to provide such discipline, the heart runs amok with desires, emotions and urges until it makes living a shipwreck. Not that we should become a heartless, mental people. We need rather to become a balanced people.

The Renewed Mind

Whenever we base our lives on feeling rather than on the objective, righteous truth of the Word of God, we're in desperate trouble. The renewed mind, by contrast, objectively identifies the truth of the Word of God, absorbs it, studies it, binds the whole being to it, and then sets the whole self on a course of obedience, tolerating no deviation from its course.

Under such discipline the heart is trained to become an obedient servant of the truth, providing law with compassion, righteousness with tenderness, objective knowing with gentle intuition. As we learn this balance we become more merciful, more loving and more compassionate toward others. Personal satisfaction and happiness result from such a balance. Left to itself, the heart always turns to selfishness.

A heart running amok as the decision-maker twists all perceptions to fit its own selfish frames of reference, makes everyone else responsible for its misery *(You did this to me!),* creates delusions *(God told me to,* though He didn't) and so much more. But the heart disciplined by a renewed mind is freed to become a *tool* for *gentleness* and for *discerning* the needs of others for the sake of *ministry in compassion.*

My daughter, aged 13, came home from school in tears one day. She had been assigned to play for a year on a team with two girls who were "stoners" (known to use drugs). Overly concerned to be personally liked by others, she didn't want to be identified with them. Caught up in a teen-age desperation for popularity, her heart raced along unchecked while her mind obediently justified what she felt. "I didn't ask to be on their team... it's important to be popular... I have a right to be hurt... I'm not going to have any fun all term..."

When the heart is permitted to rule, and to make the decisions, the carnal mind becomes the enforcer and justifier of selfishness. We had a little talk together, in which I gently but insistently made her think through the situation — a function of the mind — and direct her heart to identify with the feelings of those two girls. I wanted her to set a direction with her mind and discipline her heart to see them in a different way, to feel *with* them, rather than only for herself. But the mind had to tell the heart to take that action. It would very rarely do so on its own. The paradox is that the heart is happy to function as the servant of the mind in compassion, but miserable when allowed to run amok — although initially it may attempt to rebel at the instructions it receives.

My daughter's heart felt strongly about her dislike of those girls, *but it was the function of her mind to decide what to do with what she felt, not to justify what the heart had already decided.* When we re-established righteous compassion and brought her runaway emotions under control, she was restored to happiness, and we heard not another complaint about her teammates that year.

Suppose that your mate does something that really hurts you. Anger results and you act on it by snapping back with a cutting remark. You believe you did it because you were hurt. You tell your friend who saw it, "Well, I just hurt and it made me angry... What do you expect me to do? Don't I have a right...?" But you didn't snap at your spouse because you were hurt. *You did it because you let your heart decide your course of action rather than the mind inspired by the Holy Spirit.* You used your mind to justify what your heart had already decided, rather than to rule over your inner self for a righteous response. And no, you didn't have a "right."

We're not talking about suppressing emotions. If you suppress your feelings, sooner or later you'll lose control. Emotions *will* express themselves, either in healthy ways as we share with and confess to friends, or in unhealthy explosions, sins and physical illnesses. Ephesians 4:26 says to be angry but not to sin. In other words, *feel* the anger, but *decide* to behave righteously. *You have the right to feel, but not to hurt others.* Have emotions, but let the mind decide on a course of action based on the Word of God.

The Beginning of Maturity

Maturity begins when we purpose with our mind to do right and then make our heart come along for the ride. For instance, I can choose not to snap back at my wife in an argument because my mind, steeped in the righteous truth of the Word of God, knows the truth and remembers James 1:19-20. It, therefore, instructs my heart to feel *with* Beth *before* acting on my anger, and to place her needs before my own.

> But let every one be quick to hear, slow to speak and slow to anger; for the anger of man does not acheive the righteousness of God. (James 1:19)

Left to itself, the heart is not only the most selfish instrument we own, it will also captivate every other aspect of ourselves. But when ruled by a renewed mind, functioning according to the revealed Word of God, it becomes a marvelous instrument of compassion. My heart then becomes a tool for compassion and not a decision-maker, running amok. How amazingly quickly we settle our arguments when this principle is in force!

Arrayed against us in this matter is a major shift going on in the way our society thinks. Call it the New Age if you like. New Age thinking first says to us that all is God. Therefore, by extension at least, man is God. Therefore, hidden in every human being is infinite potential because man is innately divine. In order to be redeemed and create a new order we must only realize our innate divinity and allow our inner voice to speak so that we can unfold as divine creatures. This is a form of the very heresy that got Eve into trouble! It's idolatry!

The real message behind New Age thinking is to do and be what you feel. We hear and see it on every side — in the media, in what we read, in movies, in college courses and in private conversation. Feeling is being presented as truth. As a result, we have become self-centered, asking the whole world to satisfy our need to feed our own feelings. We are being sold a way of thinking designed to subjectivize the Word of God until there is no more clear word from Him, and to unleash the heart as the master of our destiny. Exalting our personal urges above the Word of God — this way of thinking comes from hell and leads back to hell!

In this perverted way of thinking, as feelings become truth and the heart is exalted as the decision maker, the phrase, "I love," becomes a definition of feeling, rather than a purposed direction for behavior as God intended.

"Marital commmunication" — a common term in our emotion-centered society — becomes a catch phrase for my effort to cause my spouse to make me feel good. If my words succeed in manipulating her into doing the things that I think will make me happy, she's heard me. If not, then we haven't communicated. My mind has become the servant of my heart, seeking ways to control my wife's behavior for my emotional gratification.

"Turning my life over to Jesus" means that Jesus has made me feel good — and had better continue to do so! If He doesn't, then I'll conclude that "it didn't work" and my mind, wrongly functioning as the servant of the heart, will provide all the hollow sounding excuses I need for my apostasy.

"Being sensitive" means that I am easily and selfishly hurt, rather than considerate of the feelings of others. That capacity to be easily and selfishly hurt turns into warm and gentle compassion when the mind is functioning righteously as the decision-maker, set on the Spirit and steeped in the Word of God. In dysfunction, the mind provides excuses and justifications for the selfishness of a heart without discipline. It simply makes others responsible for its own misery.

"Sexual morality" comes to mean jumping into bed only with people I am "committed to." The truth is, an undisciplined heart wanted to do it and the mind provided the justification rather than serving its intended role of holding the heart to the revealed truth of the Word of God.

But since the society in which we live is telling us that we are innately divine, we concluded that whatever we felt or heard from our inner voice was the truth. The mind then provided the framework of justifications. Thus we idolatrously deify our feelings.

The problem can be almost impossible to deal with. The subconscious agenda of most couples in counseling concerning marital problems is, "Make us feel good so we can like each other again." They don't really want the truth because that would mean their minds would have to discipline their hearts to obey. Our hearts don't want to do that and our minds are lazy. So if I, as a counselor, try to make the mind of one see the others's pain and call the heart to identify with it, I become the bad guy! "You're against me!"

A young wife from a poor background constantly questions her husband concerning his business ventures. He sells used furniture from a store he owns. "You didn't ask enough for this piece... You paid too much for that one... This one can't be fixed..." He always makes money, but she telegraphs to him that it's never enough. He reacts in anger because he feels his efforts on her behalf, his sacrifices of labor and love, are being downgraded. His reaction is intensified because he hears her through the filter of his unresolved judgments of his critical mother. In the face of his anger she retreats to silence, which enrages him all the more.

The roots of the problem are clear. They can both see why they react the way they do. We pray together, forgiving parents and mouthing repentances for judgments that grew from those childhood relationships. Tears are shed and everything looks good. I then ask the husband, "Can you now understand why she reacts the way she does?" I ask the wife the same question.

Now each one thinks I have taken sides against him or her. Why? Because in each of them the mind is still justifying sinful reactions instead of directing the heart into real forgiveness and godly compassion. Therefore, in spite of the prayers, there is no healing. As the counselor, I have become the enemy because I called their hearts to account for selfishness. Neither party wished to change personally. In reality each one wanted the other to be different so that he or she could "feel good." For them, personal feelings were truth. The mind was merely a servant to provide a framework of defense for what the heart had already decided.

I can't count the times I have suffered through a session in which the couple spent an entire hour disagreeing over what actually happened in some conflict situation. "You said..." "No I didn't...It was you who said..." "You liar! Those were you're exact words!" It's almost impossible to get them stopped long enough to do some mature communicating. Each one believes what he or she is saying. Neither is consciously lying, but neither is telling the truth. Nor is either of them willing to hear the truth. Both are interested only in establishing that what he or she is *feeling* is the truth. Each wants only to be the winner at the other's expense.

Ask either combatant, "Can you understand why he (or she) is so angry?" and you become the enemy because you have challenged their sacred cow by suggesting that someone's heart might not be telling the truth, and because you have at least hinted that it might be wise to give up control. You have called the mind to demand that the heart abandon selfishness and begin to have empathy for the other. But that's hard. It takes self-sacrificial effort. It means that the heart can no longer be allowed to run amok, reacting unhindered and allowed to feel without discipline or righteous direction. It means that the mind, renewed by the Spirit, must take its rightful place as the servant of righteousness and call the heart to account. But the heart is desperately wicked, more deceitful than all else. "It's too hard," it lies, "So I'll be mad at the counselor."

At this point, the mind, serving rather than directing the heart, begins to justify hatred for the counselor. Every counselor knows that often some wildly creative versions of what has been said in counseling are passed around by sick people. Repeatedly I have called two people to account, only to have both of them flee the office to accuse me of saying it was, ". . . all *my* fault! What about him?" or "What about her?" The mind and the heart remained in dysfunctional relationship and so my statements of mutual responsiblity could not be heard. They could pay only lip-service to acceptance of personal guilt.

As a child I had a problem with moods. Not just with having them. I had to make everyone else miserable with me. When my father, and our family with him had suffered enough, he would swat my bottom and in his best stern voice command, "Now you be happy!"

Even as a child I thought, "What a dumb thing to say!" But the message was on target. "Stop letting your feelings lead you around by the nose. Decide with your mind how you will live and then demand that your heart follow along. Get it in order."

Somehow the message sank in. I can't live for my emotions but neither can I nor should I make them go away. I can, however, live for righteous actions. I can have emotions, but *act* righteously on the basis of the eternal, revealed Word of God.

Sunday after Sunday that skill gets me through worship services and sermons, joyful for the sake of my people, no matter what my heart might be feeling. I'm still a melancholic personality, still unable to generate right and positive emotions on command. But with my Spirit-renewed mind I can set the kind of direction for righteous behavior that summons my heart to give sensitivity and life to what I've decided to do. The discipline of a transformed and renewed mind turns the heart into an instrument of power and compassion. I may still be miserable in a corner of my being, but I can be genuinely "up" for my people when the ministry demands it. I can simply put my melancholic feelings in another "room" and then choose to live out the joy of the Holy Spirit in me.

(Proud father's note: since Loren wrote these words, he has had a tremendous breakthrough into abiding moment by moment every day in the presence of the Lord! His melancholy nature is gone — and he is filled with the joy of the Lord. But the advice is still valid for those who do still become melancholy, or for those times when one has a "down day" anyway.)

The Task of the Mind

In our broken thinking we really believe emotions are strength. They're not. We believe anger is protection. It isn't. We believe feelings are honest. They lie. The mind is designed to identify the facts of the Word of God and then demand that the heart obey. *The task of the mind is to provide the heart with a framework of objective truths within which to operate.* The result is righteousness tempered with the gentleness of God. It is power blessed with compassion.

Proverbs 16:32 says, "He who is slow to anger is better than the mighty, And he who rules his spirit, than he who captures a city." Proverbs 17:27, "He who restrains his words has knowledge, And he who has a cool spirit is a man of understanding." Proverbs 25:28, "Like a city that is broken into and without walls Is a man who has no control over his spirit." Proverbs 17:20, "He who has a crooked mind finds no good." If the renewed mind blessed by the Holy Spirit is not the boss, a man has no capacity to rule over negativity. Trapped in negativity, he can see no good in anything or anyone.

I believe we have much teaching to do. It won't be easy because we're running against the mainstream of our modern culture. It won't be easy because most children aren't being raised today with godly discipline at home, much less any training in discipline of the heart. We must teach persistently and expect to win few popularity contests. But if we can convince a person to agree to the struggle and stay in it, we've won. Next to receiving Jesus for the first time, that simple decision can be the most important turning point in any individual life.

> *For though we walk in the flesh, we do not war according to the flesh, for the weapons of our warfare are not of the flesh, but divinely powerful for the destruction of fortresses. We are destroying speculations and every lofty thing raised up against the knowledge of God, and we are taking captive every thought captive to the obedience of Christ. (2 Cor. 10:3-5)*

As Christian healers we aren't in business to make people feel good, but to take thoughts captive that the heart might follow after.

9

Right Thinking About the Church and Authority

By R. Loren Sandford

As a result, we are *no longer to be children,* tossed here and there by waves, and carried about by every wind of doctrine, by the trickery of men, by craftiness in deceitful scheming; but *speaking the truth in love, we are to grow up* in all aspects into Him, who is the head, even Christ, from whom the whole body, being fitted and held together by that which every joint supplies, according to the proper working of each individual part, causes the growth of the body for the building up of itself in love. This I say therefore, and affirm together with the Lord, *that you walk no longer just as the Gentiles also walk, in the futility of their mind.* (Eph. 4:14-17, italics mine)

This chapter was given originally as a teaching at an Elijah House seminar entitled "The Renewal of the Mind," in Spokane, Washington, in October, 1987. I went into that teaching with a bare minimum of notes, uncertain of what I would be saying, knowing only that the Lord had led me to "shoot from the hip" and trust His Spirit for guidance. What came out was an impassioned plea to the Body of Christ to grow up and change its immature patterns of thinking about relationships among brothers and sisters.

In the writing of this chapter I hope to preserve some of the spontaneous and passionate flavor of that anointed moment. More than imparting information, I want to communicate a new attitude, a new intensity of love for the glory of this messy miracle we call "the Church."

In considering the broken, unbiblical thinking so many of us do concerning the Body of Christ and authority, I am led again to the problem of the inversion of the roles of mind and heart. Again I see the mind too often serving the heart to justify what the heart feels rather than functioning as it ought in understanding the truth, making decisions and setting parameters. Our thoughts about the Body of Christ and about authority too frequently *reflect* our feelings and judgments, rather than determining them according to God's Word.

Rugged Individualism

Let's begin with our broken thinking concerning the Body of Christ. *Our Anglo-American tradition of rugged individualism* was great for the frontier. Rugged individualism goes back hundreds of years and helped us explore a continent and build a nation, but it can be a poison to the Body of Christ. "I'm going to go into the wilderness, away from people, and I'll build my own place there with no help from you, thanks! And when it gets too crowded, I'm going to move farther out and I'm going to be an entrepreneur and

I'm going to build my own empire and it's going to be all mine and I'm a self-made man!" How deeply rooted in our culture is that attitude! And so common, even among servants of the Lord!

Therefore, the fact that we believers are baptized *by the Spirit into one Body* (1 Cor. 12:13), doesn't find a lodging place in our understanding. Too many of us don't comprehend it because we've missed what it means to be corporate, one with others. Instead of the mind then seeking to comprehend what this passage really implies in terms of commitment and behavior, it justifies what the heart has already told us, "I'm just a rugged individualist and I can have faith on my own, and I can worship Jesus on my own. Of course, I believe in Christ! I don't need to go to church to believe in Christ!"

That's rotten thinking, not because it isn't true, but because it's misapplied — right thoughts justifying wrong attitudes and actions. It's true that I can have faith in Him without going to church. But it is sin to use those truths as justifications for avoiding fellowship. When we think that way, the mind is serving what the heart already believes, rather than binding all to the Word of God.

Many of us are children of divorce and the numbers are increasing. In such persons often the concept of wholesome, healthy corporateness has been shattered. They're not going to risk emotional vulnerability. They're not going to truly commit themselves anywhere or let themselves become a part of anyone else's flow.

I was raised in a whole family, the oldest of six children. I knew that mom and dad were permanent, that if the world blew up tomorrow, "mom-and-dad" would still be one word. I also learned that I couldn't sleep in the same bedroom with three brothers without learning to give. In those crowded quarters I was forced to take some of the rough edges off my own behavior so that I could guarantee myself survival. With discouraging regularity my brothers broke things that belonged to me, and so I *had* to learn to forgive. At least once a week I brushed my teeth with a wet toothbrush because someone else had used it! I had no choice but to learn to let all that go by for the sake of the peace of the whole.

Mom and dad were never very secret about their arguments, although I'm certain they thought they were. We could see mom's frustration blossom as thirty minutes grew to an hour and still there was no sign of our father home for supper. I can still hear her muttering to herself in mounting anger as she held dinner for the whole family and asked us kids to, "Send thoughts at your father." No occult practices here. Just an angry joke.

We all knew something was amiss because of the way her frustration showed. But we also saw that as soon as dad was through sinning by being late and she was through sinning back at him in her frustration, they hugged each other and forgave. We learned important lifetime skills by witnessing both the tension and the inevitable resolution.

All of these situations were precious practical lessons in corporateness. They were instruction in how to be one with others without ceasing to be myself, in how to live in a covenant household made up of people from whom God will not let me escape. Life with three brothers and two sisters taught me to do whatever had to be done to resolve conflicts without selling myself out. No matter how hard we fought, we were still family and always would be.

Children of Divorce and Absentee Parents

Divorces *shatter* that built-up trust. Children usually come out of it so wounded that something in them says, "I will never be one with another human being again. I won't risk that." Then, when confronted with the call to become one with another family, the Body of Christ, the same inner voice says, "I'm not going to risk it." They're not going to involve the real self. They'll be excited for a while by the presence of the Lord in worship and by the warmth of the fellowship, but as soon as things get down to the real "nitty gritty" — when there's an argument, or when someone's personality or behavior really stinks — they leave because it isn't fun anymore. They have too few skills in oneness with others. Tragically, they don't know how to embrace the crucible of relationships that produces sanctification.

An increasing number of us are being raised by absentee parents — even when our families stay together. I can understand when both the mother and father of families with small children must work outside the home. In some cases a double income is necessary just to feed and clothe the family properly, but I strenuously object when both parents choose to work in order to support affluence. Already our society reaps the whirlwind for this sin against our children's security.

Our rising crime rate and escalating number of divorces are both indicative of the destruction our modern societal patterns are bringing on us. Children have watched their parents pursuing materialistic, self-oriented priorities and *have learned that commitment to relationships is less important than possession of things.*

Children are too often left on their own while parents are away all day, and in that environment of loneliness, they work through life's obstacles without the guidance of those whose years have given them understanding of life's experiences needed for balance in a child. Even when children are placed in a good day care situation, those who mean the most — mom and dad — aren't present.

A child then faces critical obstacles and important milestones by himself until somewhere in his heart he determines, "Authority doesn't look out for me so I'm not ever going to *let* authority look out for me. I'm not going to be corporate with anybody! I'm on my own and, by God, I'm going to *be on my own.* You weren't there when I needed you; I'm not ever going to let you be there! I'll never risk needing others again!"

I'm describing what the heart takes hold of, because sooner or later the dysfunctional carnal mind obeys the heart and justifies its fears and resolutions.

The Passive Generation

We are the passive generation. I'm ashamed to say that my household has four active television screens in it. My wife and I therefore frequently find ourselves running "basement patrol" — where we keep our big screen — kicking children out so that they won't become "couch potatoes." We of the post-war baby boom are the first of the *TV generation, trained to receive passively, to be entertained rather than actively participate in and affect life.* We're lazy, mentally and emotionally.

Since I pastor a church in which the average member's age lies between thirty-five and forty, I can speak with authority. By and large, we don't know how to give of ourselves consistently or participate effectively *with* others in collective endeavors. It's too much work. It's easier to sit and be fed, to have all the work done *for* us. As a result, we're a society of church hoppers and "lone stranger" Christians seeking one source of spiritual entertainment after another, erroneously calling our meanderings "the leading of the Lord."

Many of the largest churches in our nation border too closely on becoming mere weekly spectator events where polished professional entertainers make it work. In many such churches, too little discipleship goes on during the week. Our generation doesn't know how to be corporate in the church or in any other setting because we've learned to be corporate only with the television set or with someone who adequately entertains us while we sit idly watching.

In all of this the mind does not become the direction-setter or that which disciplines our inner urges, but rather the servant of the heart, obediently justifying and fortifying whatever the heart is feeling. So we come up with all kinds of excuses for not being corporate and for not being fully a part of a local expression of the Body of Christ. Some of these excuses sound like they were invented by fine minds and some are just plain stupid. All of them are heresy straight from hell.

One of the worst lines I've heard is, "The church is full of hypocrites, so I just can't be there." Whenever I hear this excuse, I want to shake the speaker and say, "You're the biggest hypocrite of all! You prideful Pharisee! If you want to be an honest Christian, then learn what it means to forbear. Learn what it means to forgive. Learn what it means to walk with the broken and the lost, and to include yourself among the sinners. How dare you separate yourself from God's people as though you were better than they!" That excuse doesn't hold water in the kingdom of heaven, and it will never stand up before the Lord's throne.

Another popular excuse is, "The pastor doesn't talk to me, so I'm never going back." It may be that I will hear this statement more and more the larger my church becomes. It seems to me a very selfish and immature thing to say. Another form of the same objection is, "The pastor never came to visit me." But is that what the pastor is called to do? Or should the ministry be a function primarily of the Body of Christ, leaving the pastor free to be the teacher and equipper he is called to be in Ephesians 4:11ff? I don't hear the Scriptures saying very loudly that the pastor should be consumed with taking care of all the individuals in the church, one on one. What I hear is that the pastor should be an equipper who trains the saints to do the work of ministry (Eph. 4:11ff). Pastors aren't called to do the front-line ministry, except as they take others along to train them in it. "The pastor didn't visit me," is just another excuse invented by carnal minds to justify unwillingness to be one with the Body of Christ.

Another excuse I've heard is, "I just can't find a place where I'm comfortable." Where did the Word of God ever lead us to believe that a church should be a place where we feel "comfortable"? Glory to God if it is comfortable, but the point of kingdom living and of union with Christ is to learn to love sinners as Christ did by laying down our lives for them. Although it can be deeply satisfying, seldom have I known such work to be comfortable.

Babies need to be comfortable, but mature persons in the Spirit need to be doing ministry. Those who buy into that objection usually mean that they don't feel comfortable submitting themselves anywhere to anyone. They're not going to be one with *any* group of people, nor do they truly want to find a place of commitment to corporateness. Their carnal minds make up excuses for what their hearts already have felt.

The silliest objection of all comes in varying forms but usually sounds something like, "I don't come to church because I can worship on a mountaintop better than I can in church!" Whenever I hear that excuse, I want to retort, "Then why aren't you out on some mountaintop each and every Sunday morning?" Let's have a little *integrity* in our rebellion! If I were to visit on any given Sunday morning in the home of one who makes such an objection, I'd probably find him there watching football rather than worshiping God on a mountaintop — or anywhere else. Furthermore, Hebrews 10:23-25 admonishes:

> Let us hold fast the confession of our hope without wavering, for He who promised is faithful; and let us consider how to stimulate one another to love and good deeds, *not forsaking our own assembling together,* as is the habit of some, but encouraging one another; and all the more, as you see the day drawing near.

Balancing Our Corporate and Private Worship

How can we possibly be about the business of encouraging our brothers and sisters in the Lord when we're alone on a mountaintop? Understand that I, myself, worship the Lord alone on mountaintops from time to time. There's nothing wrong with spending private, personal time with God. In fact, we need a balance of corporate and private worship in order to be spiritually healthy. But we run off the track when our private personal worship is used as an excuse to avoid commitment to corporate worship and fellowship with others in the Body of Christ. Corporate worship with other believers on the Lord's Day in the Lord's House is a divine command and *therefore constitutes a moral issue.* Let's learn to *think biblically and to bind our hearts to biblical truth.*

"Well, I'm just part of the universal Body of Christ and I attend lots of different churches! I'm just a kind of a prophet to all these churches and I really can't join any particular one." Do you know what pastors think of one who claims to be a prophet to all these different churches? Something like, "Oh, dear Lord! Here he comes again!"

Such "prophets" don't visit my church very often anymore because we don't allow them to speak. They understand nothing of corporateness nor of submission to local authority — nor do they wish to. What they really want is to exalt themselves at others' expense, and to condemn those who won't listen to them. Their hearts are sin-filled in relation to the Body of Christ and their minds find ways to justify their sin. They go from place to place bloodying sheep with phony and often condemning words because that makes them feel important. The messages they give actually reflect judgments in their own hearts rather than reality or the eternal Word of God. "Beware of the false prophets, who come to you in sheep's clothing, but inwardly are ravenous wolves. You will know them by their fruits" (Matt. 7:16a).

Time for Bible study. What does the Word of God have to say concerning our oneness and our functioning together? It's important to know the answer because *the mind is renewed largely by feeding it the pure Word of God until our thinking processes conform to those of the Scriptures.*

Scripture expresses the mind of Christ all believers have received. The passage is Ephesians 4, starting at verse 11. "He gave some as apostles [church planters and builders], and some as prophets [building inspectors and watchmen on the wall who see what the Lord is doing and pray for it, sometimes speaking publicly], and some as evangelists [for the bringing in of new believers], and some as pastors and teachers [two offices for caring for the sheep], for the equipping of the saints for the work of service, to the building up of the Body of Christ."

Artists in Ministry

In the original Greek the word for "equipping" is *katartis*. *Kata* is a prefix intensifying whatever it's attached to. *Artis* is related to our word "artist." It is therefore the task of leaders in the Body of Christ to make the saints into consummate artists in ministry, to equip believers in such a way that they become supremely skilled artisans in the "work of service." I've learned that when I'm doing front-line ministry in my church, I'm often taking it away from some layperson who should be doing it — unless I have others with me to be trained. I'm not called to do the ministry but *to train others in it.*

"Building up" comes from a word in the original Greek that derives from *oikodome* (oy-koh-doh-may). The meaning of *oikodome* is "house" or *"household,"* so that the phrase, "building up," means not just that the Body of Christ grows larger, and not merely that the individuals in it become stronger, but that it becomes a household in strength.

"Lone-Stranger" Christians

In my heart a household was where two parents and six kids lived without the right to run away from one another, where we learned what it took to live in some semblance of peace because for us *there were no other options.* By disciplining ourselves to read this passage as Paul structured it, one concept depending upon the previous for its fulfillment, we see that the Body of Christ becomes a household in strength *only by working together at the task of ministry.*

How in heaven's name are we going to participate in that process as "lone stranger" Christians? Whatever the excuses for avoiding covenant commitment to a local expression of the Church, they're invalid. God has called *all* of us to become skilled artisans in the Body of Christ, working intimately with brothers and sisters in the Lord until we become a household with hearts beating as one, given to the ministry and to one another.

I discovered how this process works in a worldly way while performing professionally as a rock musician during my high school years. The group I worked with learned to play our instruments as beginners together, and for four years we traveled across three states and two provinces of Canada. Before those four years ended, we knew one another so well we could "jam" for an hour and a half, non-stop, totally unrehearsed, instinctively knowing where the music was going without even looking at one another. This had become possible because of the many hours we had spent together, working at our music, each of us committed to the common goal.

The Body of Christ ought to be like that, only more wondrously so because the power of the Holy Spirit draws us together and makes our music! *It's the work we share in the Holy Spirit that binds our hearts together!* Not the pastor's love, taking care of the sheep, one by one. Not whether your small group treated you rightly. Not compatible personalities. But *did you work together at this marvelous task of building up the Body of Christ?* Were you struggling for the gospel as one with your brothers and sisters? Is there anything more important to be doing?

As a couple, my wife Beth and I lay no other obligation on one another than that we work together, partners in the ministry. She's not *obligated* to make me happy or to perform for me in any way, nor I for her, though in Jesus we do try to bless and please one another. *The glue that binds us together and keeps our marriage on track isn't based on our capacity to make each other feel good.* We're thankful for that because sometimes we don't make one another very happy!

What binds us together and keeps us communicating and growing in the same direction is the work we perform together for the sake of the Gospel. *The task we accept and pursue together builds us into a household.* We understand that sometimes through no fault of the one, both are not united as one in serving Christ — but the point is not about earthly marriage. I testify about Beth and me as a parable of that greater marriage which is the Lord and His Church. Again I say, *the task we accept and pursue together as a people builds us into a household.*

Covenantal Commitment

"Until we all attain to the unity of the faith, and of the knowledge of the Son of God" (Eph. 4:13). We become a household in the church because of joint labors, and the result is unity. Unity in turn brings us to a more complete knowledge of the Son of God. On the basis of Ephesians 4:13, I'm going to make a statement to which some in the past have responded in anger. If you don't agree with me, then I submit that you have the clear meaning of God's Word to argue with.

Beyond spiritual infancy, no Christian can know Jesus without being committed to working with other Christians in covenant as part of a specific local expression of the Body of Christ. A covenant is an agreement I make with *God* in relation to you. It is not an agreement we make *with one another* to bind and imprison one another. Apart from commitment as outlined in Ephesians 4, you may know Him as a baby knows its mother, but you will never attain to a truly adult relationship *with* Him.

Children don't really "know" their parents. They lack the wisdom and perception that come only from years of living and experiencing. My father and I can labor together in the writing of this book, hashing out our disagreements in harmony, because we know one another through years of serving together in harness for the Lord *in our adulthood.* The kinds of experiences that enable any of us to know Jesus in a mature way are found only in covenant with other believers as we work together for the sake of the Gospel.

Apart from such involvement we might come to know a mere idea *about* Jesus, or some sentimental *feeling* about Him, but we won't *know Him.* We truly know Him only as we have lived and labored *with* Him. *But we only labor with Him and dwell in His household as we work and live with other believers as part of a local expression of the Body of Christ.*

The second half of Ephesians 4:13 reads, ". . . to a mature man, to the measure of the stature which belongs to the fulness of Christ." People have actually said to me, "I'm just too mature for any church I've been in." What arrogance! I want to shout, "Brother, you don't understand anything! There *is* no maturity until you've learned to work with others and come to unity so that you know Jesus."

Romans 15:1 defines maturity for us, "Now we who are strong ought to bear the weaknesses of those without strength and *not just please ourselves.*" These people in their arrogance seem to have missed those Scriptures which say, "For if anyone thinks he is something when he is nothing, he deceives himself" (Gal. 6:3), and "Be of the same mind toward one another; *do not be haughty in mind,* but associate with the lowly. *do not be wise in your own estimation"(Rom. 12:16, italics mine).*

Ephesians 4 continues through verse 16:

> As a result, we are no longer to be children, tossed here and there by waves, and carried about by every wind of doctrine, by the trickery of men, by craftiness in deceitful scheming; but speaking the truth in love, we are to grow up in all aspects into Him, who is the head, even Christ, from whom the whole body, being fitted and held together by that which every joint supplies, according to the proper working of each individual part, causes the growth of the body for the building up of itself in love.

Find me a reason for avoiding involvement in a local church that can stand up to that Scripture! We need to feed our dysfunctional minds on this kind of Word so that our renewed minds can provide godly bounds within which our hearts can be made to thrive. *Don't tell me you're a biblical Christian if you're not committed to a local church!* Let's learn to think rightly — and that means *biblically only!*

Accepting Differences

How about this one? "Well, I just can't agree with everything they believe!" Read Romans 14. Paul addresses those who are arguing about worship days and what kinds of foods Christians ought or ought not to eat. According to Sandford's twentieth-century paraphrase, Paul is saying, "I don't care what day you worship on! I don't give a rip what you eat! Let every man be convinced in his own mind that he is doing what God has called him to do. But in your freedom to choose, be careful not to cause your brother to stumble. Whatever choices you make, do what you do as to the Lord *and stop judging others for their convictions.*"

Minor doctrinal differences are unimportant. We are to come together in and for the person of Jesus, and we are to do all things for His glory. God doesn't ask that you agree with everything your church does or believes, but He does ask that you be invested in serving and that you do it for Him. Above all, have enough humility not to require your church to agree with every point of your personal doctrine!

"Well, I'm not being fed!" is another mental justification for the perversion of the heart —

although very occasionally God does call a dying babe out of a place of spiritual famine. Normally, however, if you're so strong (or so weak) that you need superior food, and if you've decided not to attend anywhere unless you can find gourmet spiritual nutrition, then I suggest you may already have become spiritually obese. Perhaps you need to lose weight by exercising what you know! *Feed someone else and so be fed yourself.* Only babies and sick people have a need to be passively fed. Adults have both the ability and sense of responsibility to feed themselves and others as well.

"I'm not going to share with my small group while 'that person' is present, so I'm not even going to attend until he's gone." James 5:16 reads, "Therefore, confess your sins to one another, and pray for one another, so that you may be healed." Unless so-and-so is present? No. The Word of God doesn't include qualifiers. I see none here — or anywhere ele in the Scriptures.

What does it really matter if so-and-so misunderstands! You won't die from it. You might even learn from it — something about forbearance, patience and forgiveness. "She'll tell everybody!" Maybe she will. But is that so important? You'll survive, and before it's over she'll be the one with egg on her face, not you. The good fruit in your life will be that you will have nothing more to hide — if you allow the embarrassment and pain of it to be borne. Concealed sins will be deprived of their power over you because they have at last been divested of their cloak of secrecy. After all, what do we legitimately need to hide from sight in the presence of the redeemed? Aren't we all sinners saved by the same grace?

"It just drives me crazy to listen to all those people complaining week after week about the same things and they never change and we always give them advice and they never do anything about it and I don't know why they just can't learn! So I'm not going." Such statements are nothing less than prideful unwillingness to identify with others for the sake of ministry. You're saying, "I'm better than these other fools, and I don't have time for them." What happened to corporate sensitivities? Didn't Jesus surrender His personal urges and preferences for the sake of others? Wasn't He patient with those whose brokennesses made them spiritual pests? Are we not called to do the same?

Worst of all is when over a period of time, someone fills his inner storehouse with judgments concerning how a group or a church is functioning and then unloads it all in one great, biting and bloody "prophetic word." These streams of vituperation always seem to begin with some form of, "Thus saith the Lord," and continue with accusations like, "You people aren't following the Spirit...You aren't praying rightly...We never share in this group like we should..." It goes on and on while the assembled members of the fellowship sit wide-eyed with shock, bleeding with every stroke of the knife.

The reality of this situation is that most often the heart of the speaker has begun to judge and condemn self-righteously. Rather than demand that the heart obey the Word of the Lord concerning forgiveness, patience and nurture of the weak, the unrenewed mind produces bloody confrontations. It blasts the group with their real or imagined sins in a spirit clearly not from God. The fellowship suffers not only wounding but confusion, and reacts negatively to what could only be perceived as attack.

The negative reaction in return is perceived by the self-styled prophet as persecution for his godly word so that he develops a prideful spirit of martyrdom, "All I did was say what God told me to say." His carnal mind then cooks up whatever rationalizations justify leaving the fellowship. No receiving of correction. No courageous examining of his own fruit. No questioning whether it could have been his own fault that beloved brothers and sisters were so wounded. No true examination of self.

I believe that by and large the attitude of the Body of Christ toward corporateness and authority is a stench in the nostrils of the Lord! I don't believe that any saint of the Lord could present any of these afore-mentioned attitudes or excuses before the throne of the Lord and receive anything but a thundering, angry rebuke. *All our ridiculous rationalizations constitute nothing but refusal to be one with other sinners or to take any real risks at the level of the heart.*

The heart wants to flee, so the mind obediently provides false justifications. The renewed mind should take hold of the truth of the whole Word of God with regard to forgiveness, forbearance and perseverance, laying down one's life and serving the weak. On the basis of that truth, it should call the heart to become a tool of compassion and nurture.

Subjection to One Another

"Be subject to one another in the fear of Christ" (Eph. 5:21). What does this subjection "to one another" mean in practical terms? One thing it implies is that every individual Christian should subordinate his own personal vision for ministry to that of his local church. No church can survive with 120 conflicting visions for its ministry.

Each fellowship must, therefore, pursue one overall vision into which each personal vision for ministry fits. The same submission to the overall vision goes for the varied missions the members of the church pursue corporately. Otherwise ugly disharmony and frantic paralysis set in, like a horse whose four legs want to run in four different directions. "For where jealousy and selfish ambition exist, there is disorder and every evil thing" (James 3:16). So we submit ourselves to the local vision and adjust ourselves to fit into it.

In no way do I mean to imply that anyone should surrender his right to think in order to fit into a local church vision. I do not mean that we should give up the right to raise questions or objections. None of us should allow ourselves to give up our personal visions for ministry. *Nowhere does the Word of God grant authority figures the right to dominate and control the individual lives of members of the Body of Christ.* I insist, however, that there are certain adjustments each of us must make in order to labor effectively alongside others.

Listening to Others

Submission also means that I must listen to what my brothers and sisters have to say *about me.* For instance, it won't do for me to complain that I'm a persecuted prophet and then run away to find another place. God hasn't given me that right. I must *listen* to what my brothers and sisters say to me. God himself may genuinely call me out of a place, but only after I've listened, and usually not even then. The Book of Proverbs is filled with admonition concerning correction and reproof as the way of life, "He who neglects discipline despises himself, But he who listens to reproof acquires understanding" (Prov. 15:32).

The elders of my church have been known to order me home on a Sunday morning when I determined to be there even though I was too ill. God has called me to submit to my brothers. I must listen even when I'm accused of wrongdoing, or when I'm opposed in my plans or teaching by those who haven't truly heard me.

In listening I may find that my original position has been strengthened or refined. That's good fruit that would not have been produced had

I not been challenged. I may be falsely accused by sick and confused people, but I find better ways to say things as I listen to and wrestle with what's being said. Or I may gain wisdom concerning how to avoid leaving myself open to misunderstanding in the future. That too is good fruit.

Then there are times when the correction my brothers and sisters bring is valid. If I turn from it, I go on sinning and making mistakes. Too many of us flee the Body of Christ whenever confrontation appears, but I have discovered there's something good in it for me.

For a time we had in our fellowship a man who was bound up in a legalistic approach to Old Testament law, and he wanted me to teach our fellowship accordingly. Week by week he hounded me, even to the point of writing me angry notes on offering envelopes, criticizing my sermons. I fully agree that the Law is still God's Word and that Jesus did not set aside the Old Testament (Matt. 5:17ff), but there are problems with living under the Law as a legal system that any student of New Testament grace can see.

Our legalistic brother was wrong — again because his mind was serving the hidden desires of his heart to blame and condemn. I could have reacted defensively to him — and often did — but God has called me to submit to my brothers and sisters and has never allowed me to back off from that commitment for very long. I was therefore compelled to submit to my brother in the Lord by listening to him. As I did, I reexamined Old Testament law in a wholesome way. I learned new things; but I never would have done it without the prodding of that brother who was wrong. Through his wrongness God said something to me to which I needed to submit.

What if someone accuses you of being a critical gossiper but you know you aren't and that you haven't been? What will you do, knowing that God has called you to submit to your brothers and sisters? If you're being biblically submissive, you'll examine what you have done with your tongue, and you'll take such a hard look at it that it becomes a much more refined instrument than it was before — even though the accusation may indeed have been false. Your speech will be more "seasoned with salt."

As the years have passed and I have pondered how to become more Christ-like — how to embrace the cross for renewal in the spirit of my mind in resurrection power — I have come to treasure above all earthly things the correction provided me by my brothers and sisters in the Body of Christ. Their encouragement, their reproofs when I sin, and even their false accusations, all serve to form and reinforce my capacity to exercise balanced objectivity concerning the Word of God so that I might govern my heart more effectively with a Spirit-renewed mind. I haven't always liked what they do and say to me, but I have determined to embrace what they bring me, in whatever form they present it.

Jesus himself speaks to me and disciples me by means of my beloved brothers and sisters — and by means of the not-so-beloved brothers and sisters! No *"lone stranger" Christian will ever be balanced, mind and heart, in the Word of God.* God designed and purposed that we should be ". . . with all wisdom teaching and admonishing one another with psalms and hymns and spiritual songs . . . " as the word of Christ is made to ". . . richly dwell . . . " within us (Col.3:16).

There can be no lasting healing apart from relationships. Every covenant made between God and man and recorded in the Scriptures is a definition of the relationship between the divine and the human. Consistently, the relationship between divinity and humanity governs relationships among men. I am in covenant relationship with God and therefore I love my neighbor. Our hearts often fear relationship, so our minds keep inventing nice-sounding theological excuses for avoiding it.

Holiness in Relationships

All biblical concepts of holiness are bound up in relationships as seen in the way we treat and respond to others. Therefore, if one wishes to be holy, he cannot avoid involvement in ongoing covenant relationships. For instance, the entire book of First Peter is comprised of teaching concerning holiness. The first thing Peter says concerning holiness is that we should fervently love one another from the heart (1 Peter 1:22). Love is relational. One could say, "I don't have to go to church to be a Christian!" but how can you possibly love anyone in relationship as Christ commanded unless you're *in* relationship?

Peter went on to command us to put away malice (1 Peter 2:1). What is malice if not a failure of relationship? No one hates empty space! If we hate, we hate people! That's relationship. And if we put aside malice, then are we not *required* to return to relationships of love with those we hated?

After this Peter continued for nearly a chapter and a half teaching submission to human authorities, including everything from civil government to the structure of the home. Peter's reason for submission? That "...you may silence the ignorance of foolish men..." (1 Peter 2:15). Again, the concern of the passage is for others. The indicators point once more to relationships. Peter was reminding us of the kind of relationships we have to foolish men and of our responsibility for them.

Now that we have looked at *relationships*, the following are some areas in which our attitudes concerning *authority* need renewing. (Once again, these are attitudes and judgments the heart falls into and the carnal mind justifies.)

Rebellion

First, many of us have parents who reared us in ways that ignited and fostered our rebellion. As a result, judgments were made that authority would be insensitive and unreasonable and would not keep its promises, that authority would be abusive. Therefore, we concluded, "I'm not going to submit to authority anywhere." Our carnal minds then supplied whatever justifications were necessary to maintain the judgments our hearts had already made. Minds set on the Spirit should have set righteous directions for rebellious hearts and sought healing.

One of the more theological-sounding rationalizations for rebellion I've heard is, "I just submit to Jesus. I don't have to submit to any man!" The statement contains just enough truth to lead us astray, but on balance that isn't what the Word of God says. The Word says to submit to every human institution (1 Peter 2:13-25) and to your leaders in the church as those who must give an account for your souls (Heb.13:17). There's truth in that statement that I must submit only to Jesus and not to follow idolatrously and blindly after human leaders, but that's not the whole truth. Let's learn to apply the Scriptures in the Spirit and in the context God intended.

A third attitude of the heart reflected in mental rationalizations is, "Submission to authority diminishes me," *as though authority implied superiority.* "He's no better than I am. I don't have to listen to him!" Our society as a whole seems to have bought into this superiority/inferiority deception. Multitudes are falling into it and living its destructive effects as though it were a contagious disease. It's one of the roots from which we seem to be compelled to knock our leaders down.

Godly authority means that authority serves and lays down its life for those in its care. Second, it means that *authority has nothing to do with value of persons,* but only with position and order and with anointing from the Lord by grace. We honor authority figures, therefore, as other sinners like ourselves, saved by grace. They are normal human beings who just happen to be called to occupy sensitive positions where mistakes stand out in bold relief. That at least deserves a little compassion!

A fourth attitude springs from the fact that many of us were abused as children in our parental homes. Abused children often will not allow authority to protect or defend them, much less exercise authority over them — even in childhood. The judgment is, "Authority will violate me, so I'm going to do everything I can to circumvent and make authority look foolish. I'm going to declare war on authority until I can produce reactions that prove how foolish authority is."

Let an inner vow like that loose in a church and see what disaster results! Once a body of Christ becomes invested in trying to prove its leadership is unrighteous, all manner of carnage becomes inevitable. Holy and righteous men can be destroyed in a very short period of time, along with a number of innocent sheep whose faith suffers shipwreck in the ensuing confusion and disillusionment.

We've become a society that cannot see leaders as human beings. How morbidly gleeful we are at the discovery of past sins in a leader's life! While our basic morality as a people has deteriorated to the point that living with one another before marriage has become socially acceptable, we recently drove a man from the race for the presidency because we saw a woman on his lap who was not his wife! (I don't believe immoral people should occupy the White House. I merely point out our hypocrisy and inconsistency.)

At the same time that marijuana has become generally accepted as a "safe" recreational drug (which it isn't), we declared a potential Supreme Court judge to be unfit for office because he smoked pot once or twice more than ten years ago! If this were really born out of concern for righteous leadership, we could all rejoice, but the truth of the matter is that we call this kind of attitude "righteousness" because that's how our minds justify and cover up the illnesses of our own hearts.

I'm disgusted with what we do to leaders, both in the Body of Christ and out of it. As I was writing this chapter, my father reminded me of a time when President Reagan appeared on a national talk show, discussing an imminent summit conference and his hopes for disarmament agreements with Mr. Gorbachev. Immediately, many arch-conservatives disagreed with his attempts, which was their right, but some of these men went on to call him names, and proclaimed him "a weak man with a strong wife." That kind of disrespect for leadership is entirely reprehensible and a shame upon our nation!

Pastoral burnout has become epidemic in the last decade or so, and the lion's share of the blame must rest on the Body of Christ for its sick attitudes concerning authority. It is as if we can't feel safe unless we can find something to use against our leaders. I can think of no national or local authority figure in or out of the Church who has been exempt from this kind of pressure. We've become so sick with attitudes of dishonor towards authority that if no legitimate sin or character flaws can be found, we fabricate some and use them to weaken the position of anyone in authority.

This is one way of obtaining a sense of control over anyone who occupies a position of power. We set up unreasonable demands and then hate our leaders because of their inability to meet them. We set them on pedestals and hate them for being there. Then our carnal minds, as sinfully obedient servants of the heart, decide the leaders are unrighteous because they can't meet our demands. Our hearts find or invent faults and our pharisaical minds provide frameworks of justification.

A group of people in the early years of our church had such a need to bring me down. In one episode of attack, they began with the premise that a pastor should care for the sheep; but their list of what a caring pastor should do included the requirement that he know *all* of the children of *all* of his parishioners *by name.* I've never been good with names and I never could keep all the children straight. That was the justification these people needed for concluding that I didn't care for the flock and was, therefore, a bad shepherd! "Our pastor doesn't know all the children's names. Therefore, he doesn't love us." My father was declared a rebel and a bad pastor because he didn't always wear black socks beneath his pulpit robe! And he worked in his garden with bare feet — "of all things!" *Any pretext will do to bring the pastor down!*

Any pastor is a human being with human limitations. If he doesn't relate well to certain kinds of people, then you have a choice. You can do whatever your heart dictates and condemn him, while you justify condemnation with your unredeemed mind, or you can direct your heart to ask, "Why does he have that trouble? How can I understand him? How can I honor him and maximize his position? How can I make my heart into an instrument of compassion for him as authority over me?"

Because we haven't learned to rule our hearts with renewed minds in our relationships to authority figures, we've lost our own ability to exercise authority wholesomely over others. We often end up doing it in the strength of our own unredeemed emotions rather than in the righteousness of God's Word. Authority can be properly exercised only when the renewed mind objectively recognizes truth and calls the heart into actions consistent with that truth. *Authority becomes domination and control of others when the mind cannot or will not order the heart to die for others' sakes.* Left to itself, the heart invariably seeks to manipulate others for selfish ends. The carnal mind supplies the means of doing so.

There are those who confuse anger with strength and so yell at their families or dominate them with outbursts of rage, thinking they're exercising their God-ordained mandate to lead. *They confuse strong feelings with authority or power.*

When the family doesn't respond to this approach, they become more angry, and employ their unredeemed minds to justify their behavior by protesting, "I try to be gentle, but they don't respect anything I say." That's a lie. Respect was withheld because they too often exercised their authority in anger. *Authority can be exercised in a healthy way only when the heart is obedient to the renewed mind functioning properly as the decision-maker, calling the heart to become a tool for compassion.*

Feelings are not truth. Truth is the objective reality of God's Word shedding light on events in the real world. Truth is God's Word which says that "the anger of a man does not work the righteousness of God" (James 1:20). Bind the heart to that truth. Make it obey by choosing righteous behavior, whether you are under authority or in authority.

Section 3
The Solution

10
According to Thy Word

How can a young man keep his way pure? By keeping it according to Thy word. With all my heart I have sought Thee; do not let me wander from Thy commandments. Thy word have I *treasured* in my *heart,* that I may not sin against Thee. (Ps. 119:9-11, italics mine)

Thy testimonies are wonderful; therefore my soul observes them. The unfolding of Thy words gives light; *it gives understanding to the simple. I opened my mouth wide and panted, for I longed for Thy commandments.* Turn to me and be gracious to me, after Thy manner with those who love Thy name. *Establish my footsteps in Thy word,* and do not let any iniquity have dominion over me. Redeem me from the oppression of man, that I may keep Thy precepts. *My eyes shed streams of water, because they do not keep Thy law.* (Ps. 119: 129-136, italics mine)

Finally, brethren, whatever is true, whatever is honorable, whatever is right, whatever is pure, whatever is lovely, whatever is of good repute, if there is any excellence and if anything worthy of praise, *let your mind dwell on these things.* (Phil. 4:8, italics mine)

Much of the solution to the problem of dethroning the carnal mind and installing the renewed mind has already been presented. In the first chapter we pointed out that we must learn not to believe and thus revivify long-ago crucified ways of feeling and thinking when they pop back into our minds and hearts. Crucified ways of thinking and feeling *will* come back to life; but if we refuse to choose them and do not entertain them, they will soon subside. A corollary message of chapter one is that we should not enter into struggling with recurring feelings and thoughts, lest that conflict allow them to assume center stage again in our lives, but once they have been crucified, to ignore them, thus denying them life.

In chapter two, we point out that some feelings and thoughts *are* in fact what we are feeling and thinking and that we must learn to distinguish between old, dead ways and what has reality in the present. The main point of discernment is that whatever feelings and thoughts plague us from the past, having already been crucified, have no real force or passion in them, unless we give it to them by believing them and choosing to act on them. The lesson of that chapter is that the way our Lord heals ensures that long-dead feelings and thoughts *will* resurrect, and that we must understand how and why and learn to fear the heart and mind's ability to repossess the control center of our lives — that such holy fear is the beginning of wisdom.

The message of chapter three is that we must resolve to live within discipline and constant prayer. The discipline is first mental: "I will *not* allow myself to feel, think or do whatever Jesus would not." Put positively, it is, "I *will* feel, think and do whatever Jesus would." And second, that dethroning the carnal mind is a matter of constant prayer. *Not "how oft have I returned to Thee, sweet minute-and-a-half of prayer," but "sweet hour of prayer,"* a daily life not only of flash prayers but of continual intercession for others for God's purposes.

In chapter three we said that the greatest antidote to the carnal mind's propensity to regain the control center of our lives is nothing other than a life given over to constant prayer.

Chapter four is devoted first to encouraging all to get into small groups in which to become more open, vulnerable and corporate. That if we do not allow others to crack into us with truth, our deceptive minds will sooner or later find a way to reinstall the carnal in control of us. We must learn to listen humbly to our brothers and sisters in Christ.

The second import of chapter four is to call us all to self-sacrificial service. The teaching of that chapter points out that only as we pour ourselves out in service do we come to recognize and love the mind of Christ at work within us.

Section two attempts to reveal the depths of the problem of unseating the incumbent carnal mind and installing the new. Chapters five through seven expose the depths of roots and ruts, both inherited and self-made, which must be adamantly forced to the cross again and again if we are to become free in Christ to walk His way.

The message of these chapters, so often reiterated, is that mere striving to change the way we think and feel will effect little help, that all things within us must be *made* to find their complete death on the cross, *daily.* These chapters are an attempt to identify to us what are the deep inherited and created ways of feeling and thinking which we must pray to death.

Chapter eight presents a teaching by Loren to distinguish what are the functions of the mind and heart, and to show what destructive things happen when we allow the heart, or our feelings, to become the decision-making force in our lives rather than our renewed mind in Christ. Loren shows that we must learn to rule ourselves under the Holy Spirit through the dictates of our renewed mind, not by our carnal feelings — and that we do not want to undergo that discipline.

Chapter nine expands that revelation into many areas of life in our society, showing the corruptions which occur whenever we allow our feelings to overwhelm what our renewed mind knows is right in the Lord.

I have reviewed these chapters not only for the value of recalling the total picture of what we have learned so far, but in order to pose some vital questions, because we might ask, "Then, for those of us who have done all that, why can't we live Christ more steadfastly and faithfully?" Or, "What's still lacking that so few really take hold to win the battle in the deep mind where it counts?" We see so few really winning the battle against the old carnal feelings and thoughts when they resurrect. "Why?"

I'm not complaining. Rather, I put it this way to dramatize the fact that something crucial is missing.

God's Intended Impact of the Word in Our Lives

I believe there are two vital elements lacking from our discussion so far. The second will be the subject matter of the next and final chapter. The first is God's intended impact of His Word upon our lives. I realize that this statement implies that His Word has not yet had His intended effect in our lives. And that again leaves us with the question, "Why?" Or, "What do you mean?"

I mean more than the simple, sad fact that too many of us read the Bible too seldom. Of course that's true. Most Christians use their Bibles mainly as a dust cover for the table or shelf. If I could shake us all up some way to drive us into regular, disciplined daily Bible study, I would — including myself. But there's something even more important to be learned here if we would dislodge the carnal mind and conform our renewed minds to the ways of the Lord.

Look again at the first Scripture quoted above, and notice the emphases (taken this time from the New International Version): "I have *HIDDEN* your word in my *HEART* that I might not sin against you" (Ps. 119:11, italics and capitalization mine).

The Lord came along one day and did His usual refrain with me: *"John, you didn't understand that Scripture."*

"What scripture, Lord?"

"*Psalm 119:11. Let me put it for you the way you misread it: 'I have put your Word in my mind, that I might not sin against you.'* " He went on to say, "*John, it doesn't say that if we put the Word into our minds, we'll be able to keep from sinning. The Word must get into the heart, 'For as a man thinketh in his heart, so is he.'* "

That set me to thinking — rather, as Mary did, to *ponder* these things *in my heart* (Luke 2:19). After a while, I realized that all of us who counsel Christians have ministered to literally hundreds of born-anew Christians who know the Word of God mentally inside and out, perhaps better than we do, and yet their lives are a shambles!

God was telling me that it is not enough to know His Word mentally, and, I believe, wanting me to reflect until I saw that He was saying that inner healing and dedication alone wouldn't get it done either. *He was saying that somehow the Word must move from the mind to the heart if it is to be effective in keeping us from sinning.*

But as I meditated further, I realized that the Word "hidden" (or "treasured") was important, a clue to a secret of power in the Christian walk.

Finally, I had to go back to the Lord and simply ask, "Lord, how does the Word become part of the heart rather than just the mind?" His answer was equally simple: "*John, if a man merely reads the Word, even if he memorizes it, that does not*

*make it part of his heart. It is only in his mind. But
if a man acts it out in self-sacrificial service to
others, that moves the Word from the mind into
the heart."*

Again, it was time to muse awhile. We all
know that what He told me is right; it rang with
truth in our hearts. But we also know too many
who have tried hard to serve the Lord, and who
know the Bible very well, but whose ways are so
un-christlike that people shy away from their
advances! Some of these have received a lot of inner
healing. More are extremely determined to be like
Him — and yet they aren't. The Word obviously
hasn't moved very potently from the mind into the
ruling center of their feelings and inner thoughts,
though they try to serve Him every day.

As I was pondering these things, a couple
came to me. They had seen some abuses in their
church, specifically in the way they thought their
pastor related to some people in the church. This
couple read the Word assiduously every day. They
loved the Lord and His Church passionately. They
strove with everything in them to walk in Jesus'
way. They felt that the Lord had given them a word
for the pastor, but he had rejected it. When they
persisted, he not only rejected the word but them
as well, and put them out of the church.

The Lord quickly let me know it was irrelevant
whether theirs had been a true word from Him (I
suspected it wasn't). As I visited with them, since
my mind was already in that gear, *it rapidly*

became apparent that God's Word was clearly in their heads but not in their hearts. Their way was so appalling to the pastor, I could understand why he reacted as he did — I would have too. I was left with the poignant question, "Why? What's still missing in their lives?"

The answer lies in that other word from the quote — "hidden" or "treasured." It is not enough to know His Word mentally. Nor is it sufficient to have served and acted on His Word until it has become lodged securely in the heart. The Word must be *treasured!*

What does that mean? More than valued, I'm sure. More than appreciated, even than loving the Bible. It speaks something of commitment but more than that, of an experience so profound it may beggar my ability to describe it.

By analogy, making love with Paula is far more for me than sensation. It is not merely a matter of experiencing delight and pleasure in her embrace. It involves rapturous meeting and commitment to one another. There is a wholehearted giving of one's self to bless the other, and a consequential irrevocable welding of two lives as one.

Hiding or treasuring the Word in one's heart involves that kind of wholehearted embrace. It bonds the heart and mind eternally and unchangeably to God's Word until the renewed mind sighs and says to itself, "I've found my resting place, I'm home"

Treasuring God's Word is an irrevocable setting of the inner computer of one's mind, much like a marriage: "I absolutely will not have any other thoughts than these." "Here I stay; this is the death knell and rising song of my heart. Whatever I see within these pages calls to death every philosophy and thought I have garnered in all my existence, and it resurrects my mind to track forever in these ways."

That kind of seeing truth within His Word creates a paroxysm, a shudder of instant embrace and simultaneous death. There is a never-ending bonding, an eternal directive sent into the entire being, which says like Luther at the Diet of Worms, *"Hier stehe Ich. Ich kann nicht anders. Gott hilf mir."* ("Here I stand. I can not do otherwise. God help me.")

I am not speaking of a momentary ephemeral experience, nor of something mystical. I am testifying of a union, a commitment, a determination, a setting of life's course, a coming to rest for the mind which says, "I am free to ask and inquire about whatever I want, I can roam the universe of investigation and delight in what I find, but *the decision about where I will settle and what will govern my actions has been established once for all. I am at rest.*"

Augustine said of the soul that we are created in God and restless until we return to Him. The same is true of our mind. It is built with an heurism (which means ever-insistingly-seeking for eternal truths to rest in) ingrained in its very fiber. Our mind quests for truth from its inception to its ending. We are restless until we find it. But when our born-anew spirit hears or sees the truth of God's Word, *something of recognition leaps within.*

It is almost as though we somehow knew its truth long before, and like a home-coming child who has been there before and now sees his beloved grandfather's home hoving into sight around the bend, it leaps in recognition to celebrate, "I'm home. I'm home," and, akin to his parents, it breathes a sigh of relief, and settles back to rest, saying, "These are my roots. This is who I am."

Once that kind of marriage of the heart and mind to the truth of God's Word has happened, a bit more of First John 3:9 has become reality: "No one who is born of God practices sin, because His seed abides in him; and he cannot sin, because he is born of God." Of course we don't want to confuse our being born anew in our spirit with what we are describing here. What I am saying is that every part of us must die and be born anew. Within our born-anew experience there is also a dying to our mind and a rising to resurrection life within His mind.

When I completed my seminary career and was ordained in the summer of 1958, I decided that despite what my professors had said, I would believe that the Bible is true from cover to cover, that Jesus is who He said He is, that the miracles of the Bible did occur as written, that He did die on the cross and was raised from the dead and that we do in fact need to be born again. (For those who are shocked about my seminary professors, remember that it was a most liberal and modernistic seminary.) In October of that year, I awoke from a sound sleep speaking in tongues and didn't even know what it was — the Holy Spirit knew in His wisdom that He would have to by-pass my conscious mind and so fell on me while I slept!

After that I locked myself in my study every second I could spare from the duties of the parish and devoured the Word of God hour by hour, for three years non-stop. Whereas it had been a struggle to read the Bible and understand, now it leaped off the pages into my mind and heart! That blessed recognition of truth, death, rebirth and inner marriage, went on day after day, moment by moment. My mind was finding and cherishing its eternal home. Time and again, discovery by discovery, I prayed those prayers discussed in earlier chapters, "Lord, I don't want my mind. Bring my mind to death... give me your mind. I renounce what I have thought and known and I receive what I see here."

Naturally, I assumed that my experience had been similar to everyone else's. It is only lately that I have seen what has happened to so many Christians. Perhaps they had been raised in a less-apostate expression of the faith. For whatever reason, they apparently assumed that when they received Jesus as Lord and Savior, their minds had fully undergone death and resurrection into the mind of Christ.

Continuing Death and Resurrection

It did not take me long after my conversion to see that our old self, our carnal character, has to be hustled to its death again and again after we receive Him. All our books and tapes on sanctification and transformation have had that realization as their base and necessity. But it has taken years of futile striving to cause some people to hold onto their healing to drive me at last to see that just as our pestilent character resurrects after its death and must be hog-tied again and again to the cross, *so our rebellious carnal minds must also be slain and born anew, again and again, daily.*

The sad realization is that very few Christians have thought along these lines. When Paula and I have taught about the necessity of continuing death and resurrection within our minds, and I have asked congregations whether they have ever asked Jesus to slay their minds and re-gird them in His Word, only three or four out of several hundred in attendance have raised their hands!

It just seems to have been a hole in our thinking about what it is to be born anew. No wonder Christians continue to think in the world's ways, and don't even know they do! In a sense, their minds have never been fully born anew. They are still walking in the old ways of feeling and thinking, assuming that they think rightly because they are new creatures in Christ. The irony is that they are in fact new creatures mentally — positionally. But they haven't made it their own in the depths of their minds yet. They haven't gone through their own "three years" of daily experiencing death, resurrection, and mental marriage to the Word of God.

Somehow, people must come to see the possibility and the need. *Our minds must be crucified and born anew as insistently as our old nature needs to be brought through the process of sanctification and transformation after conversion.* At the deepest level, where the will arises to take hold of life, there needs to be a blessed marriage of the Word of God with the mind's grasp of life. Within all the recesses of the mind, it needs to resonate, "This (the Word of God) is reality! I will adhere to this with everything in me."

The unfortunate truth is that that kind of inner marriage of the mind to God's revealed Word does not just automatically happen. We have to invite it. Only our Lord can cause it. It is our part to seek it fervently.

May I plead with every reader? Do not merely read in the Bible — though it would greatly help if you would do at least that, regularly. But as you read, pray fervently that your own mind be brought to death on His cross, and that your mind and heart be fastened onto His truths irrevocably, to feel and think and do what His Word says. *Pray for the conversion of your own mind a thousand times.* It only takes once to obtain Jesus as the Lord and Savior of our soul; but it takes a persistent thousands of times to weld all our living to what the Word says.

Moving God's Word From the Mind to the Heart

Now let us return to the concept of serving until the Word has been moved from the mind to the heart. Perhaps the quandary can be solved. There is an answer to why my friends who tried so hard to serve the Lord had to be put out of the church because their ways were so offensive. The answer is simple — lack of death.

When they read and acted on the Word, it fastened itself into their heart, but to the *unrenewed* heart. Now, their perverted understandings of the Word only fueled their confusions with rationalisms backed up with eternal truths — "How dare you question what the Bible says! I'm right and you know it." As Loren made clear in the eighth chapter, their carnal minds busily justified what arose from the perversions of their hearts — with the finality of Scriptures to back them up!

This is why the two words must go together; "Thy word have I *treasured* in my *heart...*" Within that word "treasured" are a thousand-fold experiences of humble dying to old ruts and ways of thinking. When death of self and entropy (union with God, thus with His Word) accompany service, the heart and mind are raptured with the blessedness of His thoughts.

It works this way: I ministered to a lady beset by a pattern of rejection. Her husband unaccountably had left her. Friends had abandoned her, though she continually served as a self-sacrificial Dorcas for them, and I knew they wanted to befriend her. The Bible says that what we sow we shall surely reap (Gal. 6:7). Therefore, I looked to see what she may have sown, and discovered that her father died when she was six, and her brothers one by one left the home — and her.

She had formed a bitter-root judgment that all men and friends would leave her, and that expectation so beamed at people that they found themselves obeying it without knowing why. She confessed her judgments as sin and we brought to death on the cross her pattern of expecting that life would go that way. Her husband came home; her friends returned. Joy radiated from her face — and I knew and celebrated the Lord's own joy that His child was restored!

That kind of experience, multiplied by hundreds of counselees, bonds my heart and mind in joy and love to the Lord and His Word. I see it work, and my heart thrills to be made a partner of Christ in His love for God's children. Therefore, I love His Word, and my mind is bonded ever more firmly to His mind.

A man berates me unfairly. But I have cemented my heart and mind to the Lord and His Word. And I have treasured His Word in my heart. Therefore, my renewed heart in a flash recalls to my mind the passages pertinent to what I need to do: "Brethren, if a man is caught in any trespass, you who are spiritual, restore such a one in a spirit of gentleness..." (Gal. 6:1). "If your brother sins, rebuke him; and if he repents, forgive him..." (Luke 17:3) "A gentle answer turns away wrath, but a harsh word stirs up anger" (Prov. 15:1). "If possible, so far as it depends on you, be at peace with all men" (Rom.12:18). "Never pay back evil for evil to anyone" (Rom.12:17). "The one who says he is in the light and yet hates his brother is in the darkness until now. The one who loves his brother abides in the light and there is no cause for stumbling in him" (1 John 2:9&10). The Word guides my mind in the ways of peace, and each experience of living it increases my heart's love for His ways.

The more I pour myself out in tandem with my Lord to love others to life, and see His truths work to help and heal the ones He loves, the more my heart bursts with gratitude for Him and for His Word. As the cross brought my old ways of thinking and feeling to *death*, so now ministry in His resurrection power according to His Word brings the mind and heart of Christ daily more to *life* in me. I can do nothing but praise and thank Him for His mercy in choosing me to serve Him. He causes me to serve despite my sinful self, does it all in me and through me, and then blesses me as though I alone had done it all! What a wonderful Lord!

11

Letting God Love Us

See how great a love the Father has bestowed upon us, that we should be called children of God; and such we are. For this reason the world does not know us, because it did not know Him. Beloved, now we are children of God, and it has not appeared as yet what we shall be. We know that, when He appears, we shall be like Him, because we shall see Him just as He is. *And everyone who has this hope fixed on him purifies himself, just as He is pure.* (1 John 3:1-3, italics mine)

And by this we know that we have come to *know Him, if we keep His commandments.* The one who says, "I have come to know Him," and does not keep His commandments, is a liar, and the truth is not in him; *but whoever keeps His word, in him the love of God has truly been perfected.* By this we *know* that we are in Him: *the one who says he abides in Him ought himself to walk in the same manner as He walked.* (1 John 2:3-6, italics mine)

If you have any encouragement from *being united with Christ,* if any comfort from his love, if any fellowship with the Spirit, if any tenderness and compassion, then *make my joy complete by being like-minded, having the same love, being one in spirit and purpose.* Do nothing out of selfish ambition or vain conceit, but in humility consider others better than yourselves. Each of you should look not only to your own interests, but also to the interests of others.

Your attitude should be the same as that of Christ Jesus:

Who, being in very nature God,
   did not consider equality with God
      something to be grasped,
but made himself nothing,
   taking the very nature of a servant,
   being made in human likeness.
And being found in appearance as a man,
   he humbled himself,
   and became obedient to death —
      even death on a cross!
Therefore God exalted him to the highest place
   and gave him the name that is above every name,
that at the name of Jesus every knee should bow,
   in heaven and on earth and under the earth,
and every tongue confess that Jesus Christ is Lord,
   to the glory of God the Father.

                    (Phil. 2:1-11 NIV, italics mine)

For months now, perhaps more than a year, the Holy Spirit has been giving to Paula and me the same two Bible verses in our morning devotions, at least four or five times a month. He prompts us each day to look up Scriptures by chapter and verse number. Usually we don't know what they say until we look them up, but these became so familiar we would groan and say, "Oh no, not again. What could He be trying to tell us!?" The verses were Psalm 102:6-7:

I resemble a pelican of the wilderness;
I have become like an owl of the waste places.
I lie awake,

I have become like a lonely bird on a housetop.

and Mark 8:18:

*HAVING EYES, DO YOU NOT SEE? AND
HAVING EARS, DO YOU*

NOT HEAR? And do you not remember. . . ?

We kept praying for whoever might be feeling lonely and rejected. We thought of friends who were suffering persecution or rejection. We interceded for anyone and everyone we could think of whose condition might fit those verses. But we could sense in our spirits that we hadn't yet understood what the Lord was trying to tell us — and He kept recalling those verses to our minds again and again. It got to be embarrassing, and downright exasperating; we just couldn't hear what He was really talking about.

Then our son Loren preached a sermon about how Jesus wants to be allowed to love us. How it hurts His heart when He has so much love for us, and we won't let Him express it. That God in Jesus wants to gather us in His arms, and though He is God and "needs" no one, He has made himself to need our love. He talked about how as an earthly father, he aches sometimes to hold and hug his children, and now that they are becoming teen-agers, they don't want him to hug them as often as they used to (or they think they don't), and how that sometimes leaves him wounded and hungry for their love. He said, "God is like that, only so much more. God is wounded and lonely when we won't allow Him into daily fellowship with us so He can love-up on us."

Lights went on in our minds — and our tears flowed! How patiently and tenderly God had been trying to tell us. We were pouring ourselves out in service, and in love *to* Him, but *we never thought to take time to let Him enjoy loving us!* We never really knew He needed it. That was why we couldn't grasp what He was trying to tell us. It was too mind-boggling to think that the very God of all the universe could want and need fellowship with us just to enjoy loving-up on us! But He does. That's the great mystery and glory of His love for us; He "...*longs* to be gracious to you, And therefore *He waits on high to have compassion on you*" (Isa. 30:18, italics mine).

We had made Him feel like a lonely bird on a housetop, like an owl of the waste places or a pelican in the wilderness! We couldn't see. We couldn't hear. We had hurt His heart of love for us.

Scriptures and scraps of verses flooded into our minds: "For God so loved the world..." "*God is love*" "Behold what manner of love the father has bestowed on us..." "We know love by this, that he laid down His life...(1 John 3:16). "The one who does not love does not know God, for God is love" (1 John 4:8). "We love because He first loved us" (1 John 4:8) "O Jerusalem, Jerusalem, who kills the prophets and stones those who are sent to her! *How often* I wanted *to gather your children together,* the way a hen gathers her chicks under her wings, but you were unwilling" (Matt. 23:37). He wants, longs, to gather us into His embrace, the way a mother longs to hold her infant child to herself.

God Wants Our Fellowship

Eventually we came to see that yes, we had known God loves us; after all, He had sent His Son to die for us personally. But somehow that had gotten locked up in history, back there somewhere. We knew He loved us personally — from afar, somewhere in His heavens. *All that knowledge that He truly loves us hadn't gotten connected in our minds with the revelation that He desires to have close, present, intimate fellowship with us!* He had loved us in Jesus on the cross, and that was that.

We hadn't heard it when we ourselves quoted, "For the Lord delights *in* you . . . " (Isa. 62:4). We had mentally mistranslated it, ". . . is delighted *about* you." It seemed somehow presumptuous, or maybe arrogant, to admit the possibility that God himself delights *in* us, longs to be *with* us, that He revels *in* our fellowship.

Since that sermon, *it has been an indescribable blessing to rise early in the morning and sit down to let Him enjoy loving me!* I feel His grace and glory catching me up to himself, and I bask like a child on a warm beach in the sunlight of His love. It's so restful and easy and wonderful.

"And indeed our fellowship is with the Father, and *with* His Son Jesus Christ" (1 John 1:3). I had never heard it — *"fellowship"* — present, active meeting and embracing, "with" the Father and the Son! Those had been beautiful words — that maybe talked about history. Now they describe a present reality! They celebrate His being present and available — no, more than available — aggressively choosing and seeking me every day, giving me affectionate touches personally and really! The Lord of all life and love himself aching to be allowed to cherish me — and what a wonder beyond belief that allowing Him to express His love to me delights and blesses Him!

That overwhelms our minds and stretches them beyond the mind's capacity to comprehend in rational terms. *His love, more than all else, dethrones the carnal and installs the redeemed mind.* Only a mind renewed in Jesus can withstand the impact of such a revelation, that the God of all the universe himself longs to cherish this one little person in this tiny little earth — *me!*

Perhaps we're "Johnny-come-latelies" and most everybody else has already known these things. But I doubt it.

Let's look at the significance of this kind of loving fellowship for what we have been talking about concerning the renewal of the mind. We have been questioning why so many grasp the Word of God intellectually, and can't get it *into* the heart and *out* to where they live moment by moment. In the last chapter, we said that there is a need to "treasure the Word in the heart" until our entire inner being marries itself to His Word in commitment to live by His commandments. However, we pointed out that some can bond the Word not to the redeemed heart but to the old! Here, in letting Jesus love us, is the answer. When we let Him love us, we come to know Him. Our spirit meets His, and soaks in His goodness. We discern instantly then, and easily, when something doesn't square with who He is.

It is not enough to have fed on His love last week. As Satan poured his defilements over Eve until she forgot what she knew, so his defilements in the world erode our energies and our "rememberer" and our think-tank, until we are again subject to confusions and delusions. We do not long remain neutral. Either our roots are sunk deeply, daily, moment by moment, into His refreshing love, or they begin to quest elsewhere, anywhere, for nurture. "Abide in Me, and I in you. As the branch cannot bear fruit of itself, unless it abides in the vine, so neither can you, unless you abide in Me" (John 15:4).

When a circumstance confronts me, what determines what my heart will send to influence my mind? What deep false motives may grab my mind's thinking facilities and try to bend its logic to suit their purposes? What ensures that my heart will fetch to my mind just those Scriptures which will bless it with data to heal and help rather than to justify my carnal heart's desire to sin? What sets my renewed mind on a solidly balanced and wise Christian course as it attempts to corral my passions and direct my entire being to obey His Word? *What fuels my mind with virtue?*

Can anyone miss the answer? *My mind and heart and spirit must have been soaked so freshly in His love for me that His loving nature wells up through everything I feel and think!* We cannot manifest His loving nature unless, as He said, we *abide* in Him.

I learn that someone has gossiped and lied about me. If I am freshly come from letting Jesus fill me with His love for me, my spirit sings His love through my heart and recalls to my mind wondrous Scriptures of compassion and forgiveness. But if I have been neglecting to allow Him time to hold me in His embrace, my weakened spirit slumps under the onslaught of hate, and I find myself making up speeches, planning how to tell that person off. My mind has now become carnal, serving rather than leading my recalcitrant heart.

Paula gets under pressure and doesn't realize that her words and gestures have obtained a cutting edge. If I have been away from Jesus, I want to flee into my ice-cave and shut her out. I can feel my heart closing its steel doors. It will be a long time before I open to let her in again if my flesh is allowed to continue to have its way. I'll take perverse delight in punishing her by withdrawing and ignoring — nothing makes her madder, and I know that!

But if I have allowed our tender and gracious Lord to infuse me with His loving presence, I don't want to flee. My steel gates don't even begin to budge to close. His Spirit sends love through my spirit into my mind and settles it upon its foundations in Him. I rest securely in Him, and my mind dutifully reflects that posture in all its thoughts.

Look at it as the *necessity* for power. It takes *strength of spirit* to stand and do what is right when everything we have learned in the world prompts us to react in the flesh. Perhaps in this regard we are not much different than a car engine. No matter how expensive the automobile, how high the octane we purchase, or how finely tuned its engine, if we don't remember to fill up the gas tank, sooner or later we are going to go no further. Just so, no matter how well developed our Christian character, how brilliant our minds in Scripture and theology, or how good our emotional life usually is, without continuous abiding in Him, *our old flesh will resurrect and manifest its corruptions not long after we forget to let Him love us enough.*

We have the mind of Christ; does it have us? We have the heart of our loving Lord; does His heart recently, today, have us? We have the Spirit of God; does His spirit freshly inundate and rule ours? "Unless you abide *in me...*"

"But this is not a preaching; it's a teaching. Therefore the question from so many is, "How can we come so easily and regularly into His presence? I don't want to fill myself with empty striving. I've never yet been able to feel that He is right beside me, filling me with His love."

What we are talking about is not a matter of trying to climb past our barriers to find God and experience Him. It is the other way around. It is an easy discipline of letting Him find us. You may or may not be able to feel His presence and anointing. It would be great if you could, even best, but it is not of utmost importance. What is important is that you decide to believe that He is there, loving you, whether you can feel it or not, and that you tarry long enough with Him to grant His Holy Spirit sufficient time to permeate your entire being with His nature.

What is needful is to believe that God *is* present, *wanting* to love you, and to determine to give Him time. Not necessarily in one hunk during the day, but to realize and celebrate that He is there, enjoying every wholesome activity we do. When we greet a friend, God is in our fellowship, enjoying our reunion. When our child lifts his arms to say, "Pick me up," our Lord is in our arms, loving His child. Whenever we do whatever we do that is ". . . true. . . honorable. . . right. . . pure. . . lovely. . . of good repute. . . excellent and worthy of praise. . . " (Phil. 4:8), our blessed Lord Jesus is in it, living it in joy in us, with us.

Six days God created, and each evening saw that his work was "good." And when on that last day, He formed man, male and female, ". . . God saw *all* that that He had made, and behold, it was *very* good" (Gen.1:31). Our Lord is a Creator who delights in all that He has made.

That means He will be chuckling over us and weeping for us whether we are aware of it or not. But the good news of this chapter is that His joy and ours are greatly magnified when we are aware and *invite Him* to share life with us. The key is our *free will.* Our loving Lord Jesus is such a gentleman that He will never in any way violate our will.

When we do not know or become callous to the fact that He is present in every good thing we do, He does not feel invited to suffuse all of our deep mind and motives with His Spirit. *But when we believe and appreciate the fact that He is there, He welcomes and delights in that invitation to imbue all of our heart and mind and spirit with His love, and therefore, with His nature.*

When we know that He is in all that we do, it not only suffuses the deep mind with his Spirit, it puts a check on everything we do — "Do you like this R-rated show we're watching, Lord? Are you enjoying yourself?" "How did you like the way I told that guy off? Are we having fun?" I have even discovered it immediately influencing the way I drive! The moment my speedometer nudges above the limit, I sense His displeasure and repent as my foot lifts from the pedal; and I feel His pleasure as we cruise in righteous ways. It becomes a joy and easy to operate righteously. I want so much to please Him, to cause Him to have unmixed delight in all that I do — in my car, in conversation with others, financially, or in whatever choices I make, ethically and morally.

Knowing in every fiber of our being that our Lord's Spirit flows through each thoughtful act, through every gentle and compassionate word, every kindness, every forgiveness, takes the burden from us and brings us into rest. We apprehend the reality that "My yoke *is* easy, My load *is* light" (Matt. 11:30). Our mind rests in His wisdom. Our heart rests in His feelings. "Thou wilt keep him in perfect peace, whose mind is stayed on Thee: because he trusteth *in* Thee" (Isa. 26:3, KJV, italics mine).

This is what it is to walk as sons of God in His Spirit (Rom. 8:14), to know and celebrate that our holy and awesome Creator God is also our ever-present, intimate friend, delighting in us as we go about the simple daily tasks and joys of life.

It doesn't require vast spiritual experiences to abide in Him; it only demands that we know and believe that He is there, in us, living as us, for us, in everything we do. That awareness invites Him to share His life with ours, and our mind is thereby transformed as His Spirit pervades all the pathways of our thinking and feeling.

Let Him love you.

BOOK ORDER FORM

To order additional books by John and Paula Sandford or John and Loren Sandford direct from the publisher, please use this order form. Also note that your local bookstore can order titles for you.

Book Title	Price	Quantity	Amount
The Renewal of the Mind	$ 10.99	_____	$_____
Transformation of the Inner Man	$ 13.99	_____	$_____
Healing the Wounded Spirit	$ 13.99	_____	$_____
The Elijah Task	$ 10.99	_____	$_____
Restoring the Christian Family	$ 12.99	_____	$_____
Why Some Christians Commit Adultery	$ 10.99	_____	$_____
Healing Victims of Sexual Abuse	$ 9.99	_____	$_____
Healing Women's Emotions	$ 11.99	_____	$_____

Total Book Amount $_____

*Shipping & Handling — Add $2.00 for the **first** book, **plus** $0.50 for **each** additional book.* $_____

TOTAL ORDER AMOUNT — *Enclose check or money order. (No cash or C.O.D.'s.)* $_____

Make check or money order payable to: **VICTORY HOUSE, INC.**
Mail order to: **Victory House, Inc.**
          P.O Box 700238
          Tulsa, OK 74170

Please print your name and address **clearly:**

Name _____

Address _____

City _____

State or Province _____

Zip or Postal Code _____

Telephone Number (___) _____

Foreign orders must be submitted in U.S. dollars. Foreign orders are shipped by uninsured surface mail. We ship all orders within 48 hours of receipt of order.

MasterCard or VISA — For credit card orders you may use your MasterCard or VISA by completing the following information, or for **faster service,** call toll-free **1-800-262-2631.**

Card Name _____

Card Number _____

Expiration Date _____

Signature _____

(authorized signature)

Cut here